CW00643902

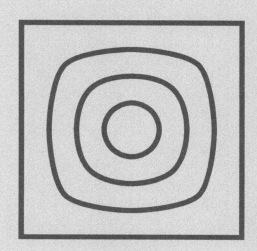

BENEATH THE SURFACE

by Shelley Husband

Crochet Blanket Pattern

US
TERMS

Copyright © 2019 by Shelley Husband

All rights reserved. No part of this publication may be reproduced or transmitted by any means, electronic, photocopying or otherwise without prior written permission of the author.

ISBN: 978-0-6483497-5-4

Charts made by Amy Gunderson

Email: kinglouiespizza@gmail.com
Ravelry ID: AmyGunderson

Graphic Design by Michelle Lorimer

Email: hello@michellelorimer.com

Photography by Shelley Husband

Technical Editing by SiewBee Pond

Email: essbee1995@yahoo.com

First edition 2019

Published by Shelley Husband

PO Box 11
Narrawong VIC 3285
Australia
www.spincushions.com

Other titles by Shelley Husband

Print & eBook

Granny Square Flair - 50 Fresh, Modern Variations of the Classic Crochet Square
Siren's Atlas - An Ocean of Granny Squares to Crochet

eBooks by Shelley Husband

More than a Granny - 20 Versatile Crochet Patterns
Granny Square Crochet for Beginners - free ebook
Flowers Abound - 20 Floral Crochet Patterns
GREG Crochet Blanket Pattern
FRAN Crochet Blanket Pattern
More than a Granny 2 - 20 Fun, New Crochet Patterns
Kaboom Crochet Blanket Pattern
Mayan Crochet Blanket Pattern

Contents

Hello!

Thanks so much for choosing to make my Beneath the Surface Crochet Blanket Pattern. I hope you learn lots and have a great time making your blanket.

What is the Beneath the Surface Crochet Blanket?

An exercise in calm, the Beneath the Surface Crochet Blanket is a solid, simple yet effective blanket for your home.

This is a project perfect for the adventurous beginner, with only the simplest of stitches used to make the solid base of the blanket. After the squares are made, surface crochet is added in a contrasting colour to make the circles and squares on top.

The blanket measures 162 cm/64 in square.

Any crocheter with basic skills will enjoy this crochet adventure. If you can make a granny square, you can make the Beneath the Surface Crochet Blanket. I will be at your side every step of the way with step by step instructions and videos available for each round of the pattern on my YouTube channel. You'll also find charts for all parts included.

You will make the several of each of the smaller squares and one large Prodigious square and, after joining them, add a simple border.

You will need

Here are all the things you will need to make your own Beneath the Surface Crochet Blanket.

You'll need a yarn needle and a pair of scissors, of course. Then there's your yarn and hook. What specific yarn and hook you use is up to you.

The information here is what I used. I have also provided some information that may assist if you'd like to use a different yarn.

Yarn

The Beneath the Surface Crochet Blanket is a very yarn hungry, solid blanket, I really do recommend you use a light weight yarn. Cotton is perfect. You see, the blanket is very heavy, even in cotton – almost 2 kilograms. If you use wool or another heavier yarn, your blanket may be just too heavy, and you will need a lot more yarn. It will also be much larger. Of course, it's up to you what yarn you use. I just wanted to make all that clear up front.

Ideally, your yarn should match as closely as possible the Bendigo Woollen Mills 8 ply cotton I used. If you are outside of Australia, www.yarnsub.com is a great website that compares yarns. If you search Bendigo Woollen Mills 8 ply cotton, it will give you some almost perfect matches that you can get pretty much anywhere in the world.

If you want to do your own research and comparison, here are the BWM 8 ply cotton properties:

Weight:	DK / Light Worsted
Texture:	Plied
Fibre:	Cotton (100%)
Hook:	4 mm (6 or G US) (8 UK)
Gauge:	22 sts / 10 cm (4 in)
Balls:	200 g; 485 m (529 yds)
Metres/Gram:	2.43 m/g (2.65 yds/g)

Hook

The hook size recommended for the Bendigo Woollen Mills 8 ply cotton is 4 mm.

Colours

The Beneath the Surface Crochet Blanket is made with one main colour and a contrasting colour for the surface crochet. You can do whatever you want though!

For my blanket, I used Bendigo Woollen Mills 8 ply cotton yarn in Glacier for the base of all squares and used the same yarn in Storm Cloud for the surface crochet.

To try out colour combinations, try the mini taster pattern on page 9.

How much yarn do I need?

To make a blanket like my sample 162 cm (64 in) square blanket using 8 ply Bendigo Woollen Mills cotton, you'll need approximately:

Main colour: 7 or 8 balls, 200 grams each (I used Glacier)

Surface crochet: 3 balls, 200 grams each (I used Storm Cloud)

If you use a different yarn or even just a different hook size, you may need more or less yarn and your blanket will likely be a different size too.

The difference in how much yarn you will need can be quite significant.

For example, this is the same pattern, made by me with the same hook. The larger blue Plain square is made with Bendigo Woollen Mills Classic 8 ply wool. The other is made with Bendigo Woollen Mills 8 ply cotton. There are 2 metres per gram in this wool and 2.43 metres per gram in the cotton.

As you can see, the wool version is quite a bit larger – half an inch bigger. It also used a lot more yarn.

The blue wool version (using weight as the basis for the calculations) used 57 metres in total while the cotton version used 46 metres in total. When you consider that this square is made 32 times, then the extra yarn needed just for this square is 352 metres. That's almost an extra 200 gram ball to make all the Plain squares in the pattern. Then add the extra you'll need for the other squares, joining and border and you can see how a lot more yarn will be required than what I used.

How do I work out how much of my yarn of choice I need?

So what do you do if you're using a different yarn?

Well, you'll have to do some calculations. First up you need something to compare to, so I have listed below how many metres of Bendigo Woollen Mills Cotton I used for each of the squares in the whole blanket. (I have slightly overstated these figures.)

4 ply (fingering)

Plain: 35 metres + 6 metres for surface crochet (38.28 yards + 6.56 yards)

Puff: 42 metres + 6 metres for surface crochet (45.93 yards + 6.56 yards)

Popcorn: 48 metres + 6 metres for surface crochet (52.49 yards + 6.56 yards)

Prodigious: 310 metres + 40 metres for surface crochet (339.02 yards + 43.74 yards)

8 ply (DK/light worsted)

Plain: 41 metres + 7 metres for surface crochet (44.84 yards + 7.66 yards)

Puff: 48 metres + 7 metres for surface crochet (52.49 yards + 7.66 yards)

Popcorn: 57 metres + 7 metres for surface crochet (62.34 yards + 7.65 yards)

Prodigious: 370 metres + 46 metres for surface crochet (404.64 yards + 50.31 yards)

10 ply (aran/worsted)

Plain: 50 metres + 8 metres for surface crochet (54.68 yards + 8.75 yards)

Puff: 57 metres + 8 metres for surface crochet (62.34 yards + 8.75 yards)

Popcorn: 66 metres + 8 metres for surface crochet (72.18 yards + 8.75 yards)

Prodigious: 456 metres + 50 metres for surface crochet (498.69 yards + 54.68 yards)

Next, you need to make one of the Plain squares in your yarn of choice. Weigh it, then using the information on your yarn label, calculate how many metres or yards you used.

If it's much the same or less than my measurements, all is well. Use my yardage calculations for the whole blanket.

If it's more, then you'll need to figure out how much extra yarn you'll need by testing the other squares as well. For the big one, as there's only one to be made, compare the differences between my figures and yours for the other squares and see what approximate percentage more is used. Apply that to my Prodigious yardage to work out roughly how much extra you'll need.

You will need to make 32 Plain squares, 24 Puff squares and 16 Popcorn squares, as well as one Prodigious square. Plus you'll need extra for joining and the border.

Help

If you just want to get stuck in and crochet, you'll find the written pattern without extra info begin on page 10. If you need help, go to the Charts on page 19, Hints and Tips on page 27 or the Round by Round Photos on page 31.

There are also videos for each pattern, the surface crochet and joining on my YouTube Channel. Search for "spincushions" on YouTube and you'll find my channel. Then look for the Beneath the Surface Playlist for all the videos.

Here are a few tips for the pattern in general.

How do I read your patterns?

If this is the first time you are using my patterns, head to my blog www.spincushions.com and search "how to read my patterns". This post has explanations of all the reasons for the asterisks, repeats, brackets and abbreviations.

Magic Circle

Instead of chaining and making a loop to work into, I like to begin with a magic circle as you can pull it really tightly closed. You do have to be very diligent sewing in your ends though, so remember that if you choose to use a magic circle.

False stitch instead of ch3 starting chain

In the patterns, at the beginning of some rounds, I have used the standard "ch3" as a starting chain in place of the first stitch. In reality, I use a false stitch instead. It is a little fiddly to begin with, but I think it looks much better. I have a video on my YouTube channel showing how it's done. You don't have to do it if the starting chain doesn't bother you. It's really ok.

Surface Crochet

This may be something new to you, but it's not tricky. You can do it. I find it quite therapeutic to do. Such a gentle rhythmic action.

Weave in your ends as you go. Trust me on this. Do you really want to have to deal with over 500 ends just from the surface crochet at the end? I sure don't!

When weaving in the ends, check your work from the front to make sure you can't see the needle before you pull the yarn tail through or you'll see your yarn from the front.

If you find your squares are still very wobbly after the surface crochet, try using a smaller hook to do the surface crochet. If you find your squares are pulled in too tight, try using a larger hook to do the surface crochet.

You will see the surface crochet yarn on the back. Here's what one of my Plain squares looks like from the back.

General Tips

Check your stitch counts regularly to make sure you're on track. It can all look fine but once you start to square off, it just won't work if you have the wrong number of stitches.

Blocking

Blocking is a little trick that helps make your work look a lot better. I do it very simply by pinning each block to a foam board and squirting it with steam from my iron. Job done! I made a blocking board myself by ruling lines on a foam mat. There are heaps of varieties of them available online if you'd rather have a ready-to-go blocking board.

I blocked my small squares to 16.5 cm (6.5 in) and the Prodigious square to 51 cm (20 in).

Ok, let's start.

Patterns

Mini Taster Pattern

This small square pattern is to help you choose your colours and have a play with a few different options.

Abbreviations

R	Round
ss	slip stitch
sp/s	space/s
st/s	stitch/es
ch	chain
cnr/s	corner/s
stch	starting chain
sc	single crochet
hdc	half double crochet
dc	double crochet
htr	half triple crochet
tr	triple crochet

The Mini Taster Pattern

Begin with a magic circle or ch4 and join the last ch to the first with a ss to make a loop.

R1: ch3 (stch), 15dc, join with ss to 3rd ch of stch. {16 sts}

R2: ch3 (stch), dc in same st as ss, 2dc in next 15 sts, join with ss to 3rd ch of stch. {32 sts}

R3: ch4 (stch), htr in same st as ss, *dc in next st, hdc in next st, sc in next 3 sts, hdc in next st, dc in next st**, (2htr, tr, 2htr) in next st*, repeat from * to * 2x & * to ** 1x, 2htr in same st as first sts, join with ss to 4th ch of stch. {11 sts on each side; 4 1-st cnrs}

R4: sc in same st as ss, *sc in next 11 sts**, (sc, ch2, sc) in next st*, repeat from * to * 2x & * to ** 1x, sc in same st as first st, ch2, join with ss to first st. Fasten off. {13 sts on each side; 4 2-ch cnr sps}

Surface Crochet.

Working from the front of the square, pull your contrasting colour yarn to the front from behind between any sts of R1. Work a ss around all but the last st of R1. Fasten off with invisible join to first ss. On back, tie ends together and then weave ends in.

Repeat for R2 & R3.

Plain Square

You will need to make 32 of these squares.

Abbreviations

R	Round
ss	slip stitch
sp/s	space/s
st/s	stitch/es
cnr/s	corner/s
ch	chain
stch	starting chain
sc	single crochet
hdc	half double crochet
dc	double crochet
htr	half triple crochet
tr	triple crochet

Plain Square Pattern

Begin with a magic circle or ch4 and join the last ch to the first with a ss to make a loop.

R1: ch3 (stch), 15dc, join with ss to 3rd ch of stch. {16 sts}

R2: ch3 (stch), dc in same st as ss, *dc in next st**, 2dc in next st*, repeat from * to * 6x & * to ** 1x, join with ss to 3rd ch of stch. {24 sts}

R3: ch3 (stch), dc in next st, *2dc in next 4 sts**, dc in next 2 sts*, repeat from * to * 2x & * to ** 1x, join with ss to 3rd ch of stch. {40 sts}

R4: ch3 (stch), *2dc in next st**, dc in next st*, repeat from * to * 18x & * to ** 1x, join with ss to 3rd ch of stch. {60 sts}

R5: ch3 (stch), dc in next 3 sts, *2dc in next 2 sts**, dc in next 4 sts*, repeat from * to * 8x & * to ** 1x, join with ss to 3rd ch of stch. {80 sts}

R6: ch4 (stch), 2htr in same st as ss, *dc in next 3 sts, hdc in next 4 sts, sc in next 5 sts, hdc in next 4 sts, dc in next 3 sts**, (2htr, tr, 2htr) in next st*, repeat from * to * 2x & * to ** 1x, 2htr in same st as first sts, join with ss to 4th ch of stch. {23 sts on each side; 4 1-st cnrs}

R7: ch3 (stch), dc in same st as ss, *dc in next 23 sts**, (dc, htr, dc) in next st*, repeat from * to * 2x & * to ** 1x, dc in same st as first sts, join with ss to 3rd ch of stch. {25 sts on each side; 4 1-st cnrs}

R8: sc in same st as ss, *sc in next 25 sts**, (sc, ch2, sc) in next st*, repeat from * to * 2x & * to ** 1x, sc in same st as first st, ch2, join with ss to first st. Fasten off. {27 sts on each side; 4 2-ch cnr sps}

Note: It will be a bit wobbly at this point. Adding the surface crochet flattens it out. Blocking after the surface crochet is recommended.

Surface Crochet

Working from the front of the square, pull your contrasting colour yarn to the front from behind between any sts of R1. Work a ss around all but the last st of R1. Fasten off with invisible join to first ss. On back, tie ends together and then weave ends in.

Repeat for R3, R5 & R7.

Puff Square

You will need to make 24 of these squares.

Abbreviations

R	Round
ss	slip stitch
sp/s	space/s
st/s	stitch/es
cnr/s	corner/s
ch	chain
stch	starting chain
sc	single crochet
hdc	half double crochet
dc	double crochet
htr	half triple crochet
tr	triple crochet
puff	puff stitch = 4hdc puff – 4x [yo, insert hook in st, pull up a loop], yo, pull through all loops on hook
fp	front post

Puff Square Pattern

Begin with a magic circle or ch4 and join the last ch to the first with a ss to make a loop.

R1: ch3 (stch), 15dc, join with ss to 3rd ch of stch. {16 sts}

R2: ch3 (stch), *puff in next st**, 2dc in next st*, repeat from * to * 6x & * to ** 1x, dc in same st as first st, join with ss to 3rd ch of stch. {24 sts}

R3: ch3 (stch), dc in same st as ss, *fpdc around next st**, 2dc in next 2 sts*, repeat from * to * 6x & * to ** 1x, 2dc in next st, join with ss to 3rd ch of stch. {40 sts}

R4: sc in same st as ss, sc in next 39 sts, join with ss to first st. {40 sts}

R5: ch3 (stch), dc in same st as ss, *puff in next st**, 3dc in next st*, repeat from * to * 18x & * to ** 1x, dc in same st as first sts, join with ss to 3rd ch of stch. {80 sts}

R6: ch3 (stch), dc in next st, *fpdc around next st**, dc in next 3 sts*, repeat from * to * 18x & * to ** 1x, dc in next st, join with ss to 3rd ch of stch. {80 sts}

R7: ch2 (not counted in stitch count), puff in same st as ss, *ch1, puff in next st, ch1, dc in next 3 sts, hdc in next 3 sts, sc in next 5 sts, hdc in next 3 sts, dc in next 3 sts, ch1, puff in next st, ch1**, puff in next st*, repeat from * to * 2x & * to ** 1x, join with ss to first puff. {19 sts, 4 1-ch sps on each side; 4 1-st cnrs}

R8: fpss around puff below, ch4 (stch), *2tr in 1-ch sp, fphtr around next st, dc in 1-ch sp, hdc in next 3 sts, sc in next 11 sts, hdc in next 3 sts, dc in 1-ch sp, fphtr around next st, 2tr in 1-ch sp**, fptr around next st*, repeat from * to * 2x & * to ** 1x, join with ss to 4th ch of stch. {25 sts on each side; 4 1-st cnrs}

R9: sc in same st as ss, *sc in next 25 sts**, (sc, ch2, sc) in next st*, repeat from * to * 2x & * to ** 1x, sc in same st as first st, ch2, join with ss to first st. Fasten off. {27 sts on each side; 4 2-ch cnr sps}

Note: It will be a bit wobbly at this point. Adding the surface crochet flattens it out. Blocking after the surface crochet is recommended.

Surface Crochet

Working from the front of the square, pull your contrasting colour yarn to the front from behind between any sts of R1. Work a ss around all but the last st of R1. Fasten off with invisible join to first ss. On back, tie ends together and then weave ends in.

Repeat for R3, R6 & R8.

Popcorn Square

You will need to make 16 of these squares.

Abbreviations

R	Round
ss	slip stitch
sp/s	space/s
st/s	stitch/es
cnr/s	corner/s
ch	chain
stch	starting chain
sc	single crochet
hdc	half double crochet
dc	double crochet
htr	half triple crochet
tr	triple crochet

Popcorn Square Pattern

Begin with a magic circle or ch4 and join the last ch to the first with a ss to make a loop.

R1: ch3 (stch), 15dc, join with ss to 3rd ch of stch. {16 sts}

R2: ch3 (stch), *ch1, 5dc in next st, ch1**, dc in next st*, repeat from * to * 6x & * to ** 1x, join with ss to 3rd ch of stch. {48 sts, 16 1-ch sps}

R3: sc in same st as ss, *sc in 1-ch sp, sc in both the 1-ch sps on either side of the next 5 sts at same time, sc in 1-ch sp**, sc in next st*, repeat from * to * 6x & * to ** 1x, join with ss to first st. {32 sts}

R4: ch3 (stch), dc in next st, *2dc in next st**, dc in next 3 sts*, repeat from * to * 6x & * to ** 1x, dc in next st, join with ss to 3rd ch of stch. {40 sts}

R5: ch3 (stch), *ch1, 5dc in next st, ch1**, dc in next st*, repeat from * to * 18x & * to ** 1x, join with ss to 3rd ch of stch. {120 sts, 40 1-ch sps}

R6: sc in same st as ss, *sc in 1-ch sp, sc in both the 1-ch sps on either side of the next 5 sts at same time, sc in 1-ch sp**, sc in next st*, repeat from * to * 18x & * to ** 1x, join with ss to first st. {80 sts}

R7: ch3 (stch), 4dc in same st as ss, *ch1, 5dc in next st, ch1, dc in next 3 sts, hdc in next 3 sts, sc in next 5 sts, hdc in next 3 sts, dc in next 3 sts, ch1, 5dc in next st, ch1**, 5dc in next st*, repeat from * to * 2x & * to ** 1x, join with ss to 3rd ch of stch. {27 sts, 4 1-ch sps on each side; 4 5-st cnrs}

R8: sc in both the 1-ch sps on either side of the next 5 sts at the same time, *sc in 1-ch sp, sc in both the 1-ch sps on either side of the next 5 sts at same time, sc in 1-ch sp, sc in next 17 sts, sc in 1-ch sp, sc in both the 1-ch sps on either side of the next 5 sts at same time, sc in 1-ch sp**, sc in both the 1-ch sps on either side of next 5 sts at the same time*, repeat from * to * 2x & * to ** 1x, join with ss to first st. {23 sts on each side; 4 1-st cnrs}

R9: ch4 (stch), tr in same st as ss, *htr in next 2 sts, dc in next 19 sts, htr in next 2 sts**, 3tr in next st*, repeat from * to * 2x & * to ** 1x, tr in same st as first sts, join with ss to 4th ch of stch. {23 sts on each side; 4 3-st cnrs}

R10: sc in same st as ss, *sc in next 25 sts**, (sc, ch2, sc) in next st*, repeat from * to * 2x & * to ** 1x, sc in same sp as first st, ch2, join with ss to first st. Fasten off. {27 sts on each side; 4 2-ch cnr sps}

Note: It will be a bit wobbly at this point. Adding the surface crochet flattens it out. Blocking after the surface crochet is recommended.

Surface Crochet

Working from the front of the square, pull your contrasting colour yarn to the front from behind between any sts of R1. Work a ss around all but the last st of R1. Fasten off with invisible join to first ss. On back, tie ends together and then weave ends in.

Repeat for R4, R6 & R9.

Prodigious Square

You will need to make 1 square.

Abbreviations

R	Round
ss	slip stitch
sp/s	space/s
st/s	stitch/es
cnr/s	corner/s
ch	chain
stch	starting chain
sc	single crochet
hdc	half double crochet
dc	double crochet
htr	half triple crochet
tr	triple crochet
puff	puff stitch = 4hdc puff – 4x [yo, insert hook in st, pull up a loop], yo, pull through all loops on hook
fp	front post

Prodigious Square Pattern

Begin with a magic circle or ch4 and join the last ch to the first with a ss to make a loop.

R1: ch3 (stch), 15dc, join with ss to 3rd ch of stch. {16 sts}

R2: ch3 (stch), dc in same st as ss, *dc in next st**, 2dc in next st*, repeat from * to * 6x & * to ** 1x, join with ss to 3rd ch of stch. {24 sts}

R3: ch3 (stch), dc in next st, *2dc in next 4 sts**, dc in next 2 sts*, repeat from * to * 2x & * to ** 1x, join with ss to 3rd ch of stch. {40 sts}

R4: ch3 (stch), *2dc in next st**, dc in next st*, repeat from * to * 18x & * to ** 1x, join with ss to 3rd ch of stch. {60 sts}

R5: ch3 (stch), dc in next 3 sts, *2dc in next 2 sts**, dc in next 4 sts, repeat from * to * 8x * to ** 1x, join with ss to 3rd ch of stch. {80 sts}

R6: sc in same st as ss, sc in next 79 sts, join with ss to first st. {80 sts}

R7: ch3 (stch), dc in next 79 sts, join with ss to 3rd ch of stch. {80 sts}

R8: sc in same st as ss, sc in next 79 sts, join with ss to first st. {80 sts}

R9: ch3 (stch), dc in same st as ss, 2dc in next st, *dc in next 6 sts**, 2dc in next 2 sts*, repeat from * to * 8x & * to ** 1x, join with ss to 3rd ch of stch. {100 sts}

R10: ch3 (stch), dc in same st as ss, *puff in next st**, 2dc in next st*, repeat from * to * 48x & * to ** 1x, join with ss to 3rd ch of stch. {150 sts}

R11: ch3 (stch), dc in next st, *fpdc around next st**, dc in next 2 sts*, repeat from * to * 48x & * to ** 1x, join with ss to 3rd ch of stch. {150 sts}

R12: sc in same st as ss, sc in next 149 sts, join with ss to first st. {150 sts}

R13: ch3 (stch), dc in next 149 sts, join with ss to 3rd ch of stch. {150 sts}

R14: sc in same st as ss, sc in next 149 sts, join with ss to first st. {150 sts}

R15: ch3 (stch), dc in same st as ss, *dc in next 4 sts**, 2dc in next st*, repeat from * to * 28x & * to ** 1x, join with ss to 3rd ch of stch. {180 sts}

R16: ch3 (stch), dc in next st, 2dc in next st, dc in next 2 sts, *ch1, 5dc in next st, ch1**, dc in next 2 sts, 2dc in next st, dc in next 2 sts*, repeat from * to * 28x & * to ** 1x, join with ss to 3rd ch of stch. {330 sts, 60 1-ch sps}

R17: sc in same st as ss, sc in next 5 sts, *sc in both the 1-ch sps on either side of the next 5 sts at same time**, sc in next 6 sts*, repeat from * to * 28x & * to ** 1x, join with ss to first st. {210 sts}

R18: ch3 (stch), dc in next 209 sts, join with ss to 3rd ch of stch. {210 sts}

R19: sc in same st as ss, sc in next 209 sts, join with ss to first st. {210 sts}

R20: ch3 (stch), dc in next 209 sts, join with ss to 3rd ch of stch. {210 sts}

R21: sc in same st as ss, sc in next 103 sts, 2sc in next st, sc in next 104 sts, 2sc in next st, join with ss to first st. {212 sts}

R22: ch4 (stch), htr in same st as ss, *htr in next st, 2htr in next st, htr in next st, dc in next st, 2dc in next st, dc in next st, 10x [hdc in next 3 sts, 2hdc in next st], dc in next st, 2dc in next st, dc in next st, htr in next st, 2htr in next st, htr in next st**, (htr, tr, htr) in next st*, repeat from * to * 2x & * to ** 1x, htr in same st as first sts, join with ss to 4th ch of stch.
{66 sts on each side; 4 3-st cnrs}

R23: ch3 (stch), 4dc in same st as ss, *ch1, 5dc in next st, ch1, 2x [2dc in next st, dc in next st], 3x [ch1, puff in next st], ch1, dc in next 5 sts, hdc in next 5 sts, sc in next 32 sts, hdc in next 5 sts, dc in next 5 sts, 3x [ch1, puff in next st], ch1, 2x [dc in next st, 2dc in next st], ch1, 5dc in next st, ch1**, 5dc in next st*, repeat from * to * 2x & * to ** 1x, join with ss to 3rd ch of stch.
{80 sts, 12 1-ch sps on each side; 4 5-st cnrs}

R24: ss in both the 1-ch sps on either side of the ch3 (stch) & next 4 sts at same time, ch4 (stch), *tr in 1-ch sp, tr in both the 1-ch sps on either side of the next 5 sts at same time, ch1, tr in 1-ch sp, htr in next 6 sts, 3x [skip 1-ch sp, fpdc around next st], skip 1-ch sp, hdc in next 5 sts, sc in next 42 sts, hdc in next 5 sts, 3x [skip 1-ch sp, fpdc around next st], skip 1-ch sp, htr in next 6 sts, tr in 1-ch sp, ch1, tr in both the 1-ch sps on either side of the next 5 sts at same time, tr in 1-ch sp**, tr in both the 1-ch sps on either side of the next 5 sts at same time*, repeat from * to * 2x & * to ** 1x, join with ss to 4th ch of stch.
{76 sts, 2 1-ch sps on each side; 4 1-st cnrs}

R25: sc in both the 1-ch sps on either side of the 5tr sts at same time, *sc in 1-ch sp, sc in next 72 sts, sc in 1-ch sp**, sc in both the 1-ch sps on either side of the next 5 sts at same time*, repeat from * to * 2x & * to ** 1x, join with ss to first st.
{74 sts on each side; 4 1-st cnrs}

R26: ch4 (stch), (htr, dc) in same st as ss, *dc in next 74 sts**, (dc, htr, tr, htr, dc) in next st*, repeat from * to * 2x & * to ** 1x, (dc, htr) in same st as first sts, join with ss to 4th ch of stch. {74 sts on each side; 4 5-st cnrs}

R27: 2sc in same st as ss, *sc in next 78 sts**, 3sc in next st*, repeat from * to * 2x & * to ** 1x, sc in same st as first sts, join with ss to first st.
{78 sts on each side; 4 3-st cnrs}

R28: ch4 (stch), htr in same st as ss, *dc in next 80 sts**, (htr, tr, htr) in next st*, repeat from * to * 2x & * to ** 1x, htr in same st as first sts, join with ss to 4th ch of stch.
{80 sts on each side; 4 3-st cnrs}

R29: sc in same st as ss, *sc in next 82 sts**, (sc, ch2, sc) in next st*, repeat from * to * 2x & * to ** 1x, sc in same st as first st, ch2, join with ss to first st. Fasten off.
{84 sts on each side; 4 2-ch cnr sps}

Note: It will be a bit wobbly at this point. Adding the surface crochet flattens it out. Blocking after the surface crochet is recommended.

Surface Crochet

Working from the front of the square, pull your contrasting colour yarn to the front from behind between any sts of R1. Work a ss around all but the last st of R1. Fasten off with invisible join to first ss. On back, tie ends together and then weave ends in.

Repeat for R3, R5, R9, R11, R15, R18, R22, R26 & R28.

Surface Crochet

How to work the Surface Crochet

Working from the front of the square, pull your contrasting colour yarn to the front from behind, between any stitches of the Round.

Work a slip stitch around all but the last stitch of the Round.

Fasten off with invisible join to first slip stitch.

On back, tie ends together and then weave ends in.

Joining

Once the squares are made, it's time to join them all into our blanket. I like to join them in strips, then join those strips together. Here's the order I joined the squares (you can do it however you want).

Looking at the layout graphic below, join the squares in the top and bottom three rows into 1 by 9 square strips. Then join the top three and bottom three strips to form two 27-square (3 by 9 squares) rectangles.

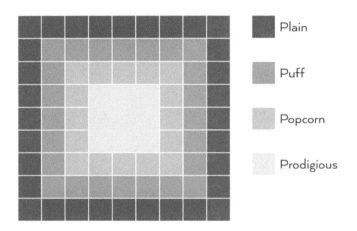

- Plain
- Puff
- Popcorn
- Prodigious

For the middle section, join three of each type of square into strips of three, then into two 9-square blocks, then join them to the Prodigious square, making sure the Popcorn squares are next to the Prodigious square (see photo below).

Joining order

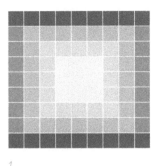

1

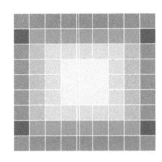

2

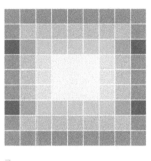

3

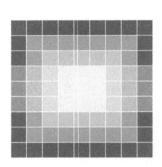

4

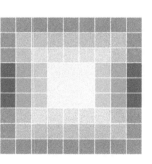

5

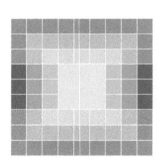

6

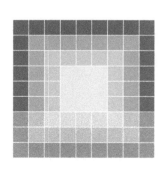

7

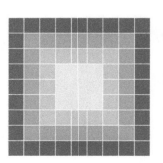

8

Joining method

We are going to join our squares by crocheting them together.

Hold squares right sides together, attach main colour yarn with a standing single crochet to both 2-chain corner spaces on each square at the same time. Work a single crochet into both loops of both squares all the way along, end with a single crochet in both 2-chain corner spaces. Fasten off.

Make sure the Popcorn squares are next to the Prodigious square before you start joining.

Once that's done, you can join your 3 large rectangles into our blanket! Make sure the Plain squares are on the top and bottom of your blanket.

You should end up with your Prodigious square surrounded by Popcorn squares, which are in turn surrounded by Puff squares and the outer edge made of the Plain squares. Magic.

Once you have your strips, here's how to join them.

The joining video on my YouTube channel shows how to join strips together, but here are the written instructions for you:

Join the strips as the squares were joined but when you reach the 2-chain corner spaces, work one stitch in each, ignoring the join. This creates a neat square on the front of the work in the 2-chain corner spaces.

When you are joining the large 9-square blocks to the Prodigious square, there is a 5 stitch difference in stitch counts. There are 5 less stitches on the Prodigious square than the large blocks of 9 squares.

Here's how to deal with that. When you are joining, make sure you do a stitch in each 2-chain space and join. You will also need to use the same stitch twice 5 times on the Prodigious square while using each stitch, chain space and join once on the 9-square blocks. I do a double stitch close to the beginning and end, and space out the other 3 double stitches roughly evenly as I go.

Border Pattern

Once you've joined all your squares, it's time to create the border.

Abbreviations

R	Round
ss	slip stitch
sp/s	space/s
st/s	stitch/es
cnr/s	corner/s
ch	chain
stch	starting chain
stdg sc	standing single crochet
sc	single crochet
dc	double crochet
htr	half triple crochet

Border Pattern

R1: Attach main colour yarn with a stdg sc to any 2-ch cnr sp, sc in same sp, *sc in each st on side, working a sc in each 2-ch sp and join**, 3sc in 2-ch cnr sp*, rep from * to * 2x and * to ** 1x, sc in same sp as first sts, join with ss to first st.

R2: ch3 (stch), 2dc in same st as ss, *dc in each st on side**, (2dc, htr, 2dc) in middle st of 3-st cnr*, rep from * to * 2x and * to ** 1x, 2dc in same st as first sts, join with ss to 3rd ch of stch.

R3: sc in same st as ss, *sc in each st on side**, (sc, ch2, sc) in middle st of 5-st cnr*, rep from * to * 2x and * to ** 1x, sc in same st as first st, ch2, join with ss to first st. Fasten off.

Surface crochet

Working from the front of the square, pull your contrasting colour yarn to the front from behind between any sts of R2. Work a ss around all but the last st of R2. Fasten off with invisible join to first ss. On back, tie ends together and then weave each end around the same colour sts on the back.

Blocking

After you've done your surface crochet, it's a good idea to block your blanket. Yes, it's big and will take a lot of pins, but it really is worth it.

I pinned out my blanket on those big foam mats intended for flooring, all joined up.

It's best to start at one corner and work your way out. Here's mine about half pinned.

When you get to the parts where the squares are joined, add an extra pin to anchor the edge a little way in from the border as well as on the edge. This will help as you stretch the blanket as you pin it all out.

You may need to adjust earlier pins as you go. Once it is all pinned out, squirt it with water and steam from your iron, paying particular attention to the edges. Leave it to dry and voila! One super-duper finished blanket. Well done you!

Charts

On the next few pages, you'll find the Beneath the Surface Crochet Blanket charts.

Plain Square

without surface crochet

Key
- • ss
- o ch
- + sc
- T hdc
- dc
- htr
- tr
- c surface crochet

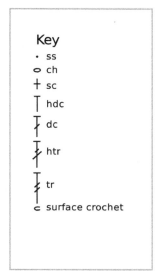

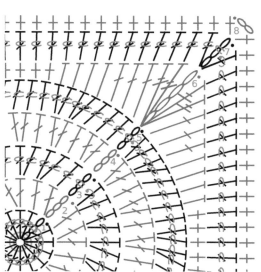

with surface crochet

Puff Square

without surface crochet

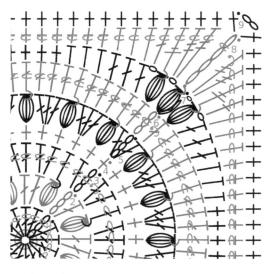

with surface crochet

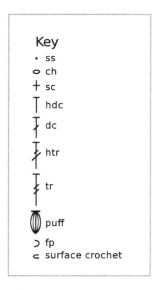

Key
- • ss
- ○ ch
- + sc
- ⊤ hdc
- ⊥ dc
- ⧸ htr
- ⊤ tr
- ⬮ puff
- ⊃ fp
- ⊂ surface crochet

Popcorn Square

without surface crochet

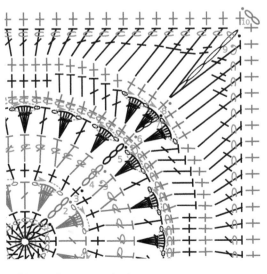

with surface crochet

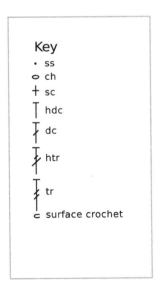

Key
- • ss
- o ch
- + sc
- ⊤ hdc
- dc
- htr
- tr
- surface crochet

Prodigious Square
without surface crochet

Rounds 1-10

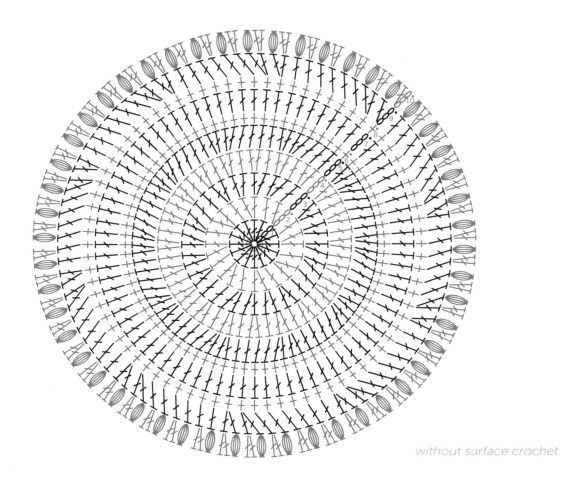

without surface crochet

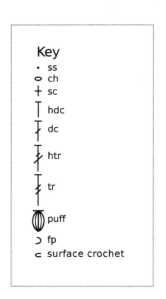

Key
- · ss
- ○ ch
- + sc
- ⊤ hdc
- ⊦ dc
- ⨍ htr
- ⨎ tr
- Ⓘ puff
- ⊃ fp
- ⊂ surface crochet

Prodigious Square
without surface crochet
Rounds 10-21

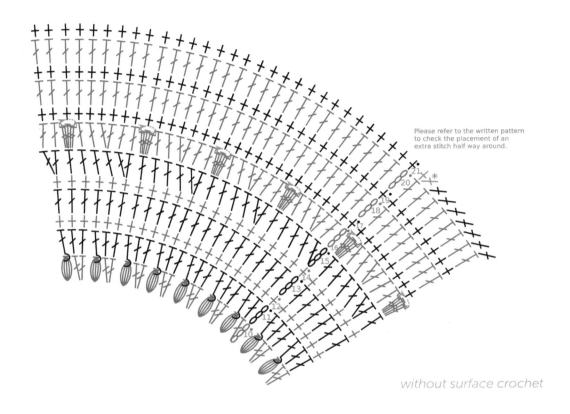

Please refer to the written pattern
to check the placement of an
extra stitch half way around.

without surface crochet

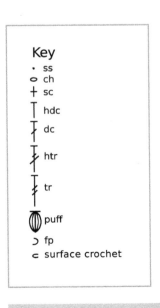

Key
- • ss
- o ch
- + sc
- T hdc
- ∤ dc
- ⨏ htr
- ⨎ tr
- Ⓜ puff
- ⊃ fp
- ⊂ surface crochet

Prodigious Square
without surface crochet
Rounds 21-29

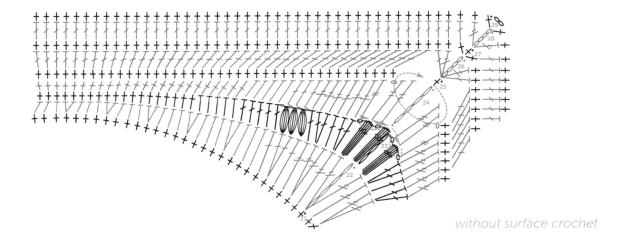

without surface crochet

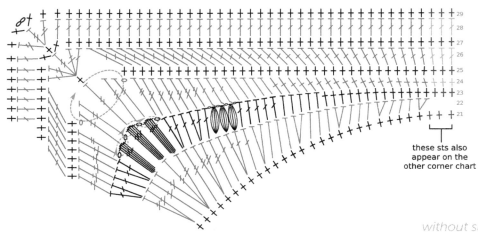

these sts also
appear on the
other corner chart

without surface crochet

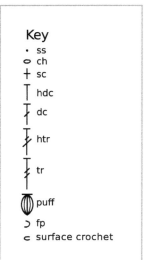

Key
- · ss
- ○ ch
- + sc
- ⊤ hdc
- dc
- htr
- tr
- puff
- ↄ fp
- ⊂ surface crochet

Prodigious Square
surface crochet

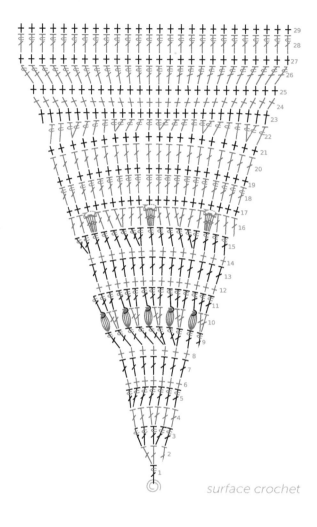

surface crochet

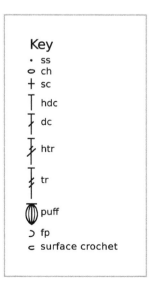

Key
· ss
o ch
+ sc
⊤ hdc
⊤ dc
⊬ htr
⊱ tr
⬮ puff
つ fp
c surface crochet

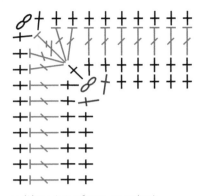

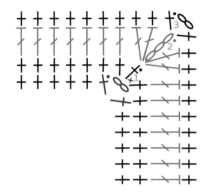

without surface crochet

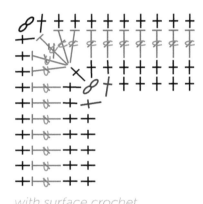

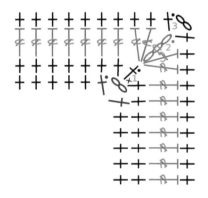

with surface crochet

Key

- · ss
- o ch
- + sc
- ⊤ dc
- ⨎ htr
- c surface crochet

Hints and Tips

Here's where you'll find hints and tips with explanations for any parts that may have you scratching your head if you've never done them before. Check my YouTube video for each pattern if you need more clarification of anything.

Plain Square

Super wobbly, not flat squares

Don't worry! Once you do the surface crochet, your squares will pull in to almost flat. A quick blocking will make them really straight and square.

This is perfectly normal! See my progress shot here? Wobbly, then not so wobbly after the surface crochet, then lovely and square after blocking.

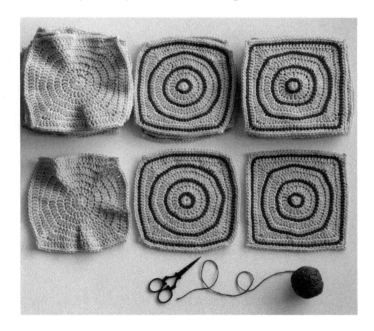

Blocking

When blocking, these squares tend to need a pin in each corner first, then a couple more on each side close to the corner to square them nicely.

Puff Square

Puff Stitches

Puff stitches can be a little tricky, but if you follow my tips, I'm sure you can do them:

- pull up long loops as you make the stitch;
- when pulling through all those loops, pull up with your hook and at the same time, pull down on your work with your other hand and slowly wriggle the hook through all the loops.

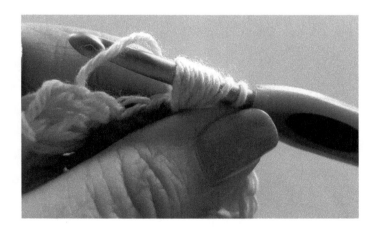

Super wobbly, not flat squares

Don't worry! Once you do the surface crochet, your squares will pull in to almost flat. A quick blocking will make them really straight and square.

This is perfectly normal! See my progress shot here? Wobbly, then not so wobbly after the surface crochet, then lovely and square after blocking.

Blocking

These squares tend to need a pin in each corner first, then a couple more on each side close to the corner to square them nicely.

Popcorn Square

Popcorn Stitches

I make my popcorn stitches a little differently to how you may be used to doing them. I do them the lazy way. What that means is there is no taking your hook out to make a popcorn. The popcorns are made over 2 rounds. The first step is to make groups of 5 stitches with a 1-chain space on either side. Then we use those 1-chain spaces to gather the groups of 5 stitches into popcorns in the next round.

The needle in the photo below shows where to put your hook to gather the stitches into a popcorn.

Here's what it looks like after the popcorn is made. Cool huh?

Super wobbly, not flat squares

Don't worry! Once you do the surface crochet, your squares will pull in to almost flat. A quick blocking will make them really straight and square.

This is perfectly normal! See my progress shot here? Wobbly, then not so wobbly after the surface crochet, then lovely and square after blocking.

Blocking

These squares tend to need a pin in each corner first, then a couple more on each side close to the corner to square them nicely.

Round 24 - how to start

We're making lazy popcorns again at the corners of Round 24 but this time we're using triple crochet to gather the stitches below.

This is where you stick your hook to make the slip stitch at the beginning of Round 24. Then you chain 4 for your starting chain or make a false triple crochet.

Then this is how you gather the other groups of 5 stitches with a triple crochet.

Round 25 - how to start

Again, we are making a lazy popcorn at the start, but this time we are using a single crochet and have to go back a bit to find the first 1-chain space to insert our hook into.

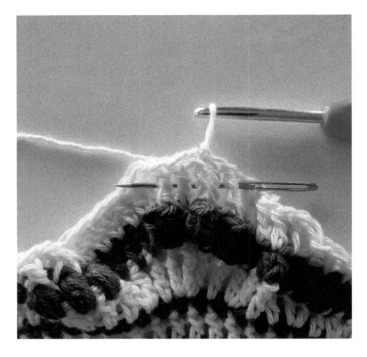

Super wobbly, not flat square

Don't worry! Once you do the surface crochet, your square will pull in to almost flat. A quick block will make it really straight and square. This is perfectly normal!

Blocking

This square will need pins all the way around. Start with the corners, then the middle of the sides and then pin as needed between the corners.

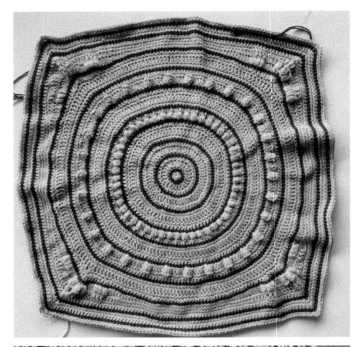

Round by Round Photos

Plain Square

Round 1

Round 2

Round 3

Round 4

Round 5

Round 6

Round 7

Round 8

Puff Square

Round 1

Round 2

Round 3

Round 4

Round 5

Round 6

Round 7

Round 8

Round 9

Popcorn Square

Round 1

Round 2

Round 3

Round 4

Round 5

Round 6

Round 7

Round 8

Round 9

Round 10

Prodigious Square

Round 1

Round 2

Round 3

Round 4

Round 5

Round 6

Round 7

Round 8

Round 9

Round 10

Round 11

Round 12

Round 13

Round 14

Round 15

Round 16

Round 17

Round 18

Round 19

Round 20

Round 21

Round 22 - corner

Round 22 - side

Round 23

Round 24 - corner

Round 24 - side

Round 25 - corner

Round 25 - side

Round 26 - corner

Round 26 - side

Round 27 - corner

Round 27 - side

Round 28 - corner

Round 28 - side

Round 29 - corner

Round 29 - side

About the Author

Shelley Husband is an Australian crochet designer and crochet teacher living on the south west coast of Victoria with her hubby and teenager in a tiny dot of a town by the ocean. Her two older children have left the nest and are spreading their own crafty and arty wings out in the world.

Shelley has crafted most of her life, trying "all of the crafts" over the years. These days, she spends most of her time with a crochet hook in hand. Having discovered a natural knack for crochet about seven years ago after a break of a few decades, she hasn't looked back, creating hundreds of Granny Square patterns.

Shelley loves nothing more than designing new patterns aiming to extend her own and our crochet skills, gently challenging and encouraging us to create timeless, classic pieces sure to be admired and appreciated.

Seamless crochet is a real passion and she has many tips and tricks to make our crochet look the best it possibly can, using techniques she has combined and tweaked over the years.

When not designing crochet, you can find Shelley teaching crochet in workshops around Victoria and beyond. For those who cannot make a workshop in person, she teaches worldwide via her annual Crochet-A-Long projects through her blog and YouTube channel.There is no doubting Shelley's passion for all things crochet.

You can find Shelley online on most social media channels as spincushions.

CPSIA information can be obtained
at www.ICGtesting.com
Printed in the USA
BVHW020937240719
554236BV00024B/1381/P

9 780648 349754

CW00643061

BOOK OF SOULS

An Illustrated History

Danann
BOOKS

Danann
BOOKS

© Danann Publishing Limited 2019

First Published Danann Publishing Ltd 2019

WARNING: For private domestic use only, any unauthorised Copying, hiring, lending or public performance of this book is illegal.

CAT NO: DAN0420

Photography courtesy of

Getty images:

- Martyn Goddard/Corbis
- Virginia Turbett/Redferns
- Ebet Roberts/Redferns
- Paul Natkin
- Michael Putland
- Richard E. Aaron/Redferns
- The LIFE Picture Collection
- Stuart Mostyn/Redferns

- Brian Rasic
- Peter Still/Redferns
- Mick Hutson/Redferns
- Tim Mosenfelder
- Karl Walter
- Steve Thorne/Redferns
- Martin Philbey/Redferns
- Jazz Archiv Hamburg/ullstein bild

- FRANCESCO DEGASPERI/AFP
- VCG/VCG
- Francesco Castaldo\Mondadori Portfolio
- Gonzales Photo/Terje Dokken/ PYMCA/Avalon/UIG

Book layout & design Darren Grice at Ctrl-d

Copy Editor Tom O'Neill

All rights reserved. No Part of this title may be reproduced or transmitted in any material form (including photocopying or storing it in any medium by electronic means and whether or not transiently or incidentally to some other use of this publication) without the written permission of the copyright owner, except in accordance with the provisions of the Copyright, Designs and Patents Act 1988.Applications for the copyright owner's written permission should be addressed to the publisher.

Made in EU.

ISBN: 978-1-912332-25-0

This book is fully independent and unauthorised by the artists their management or record company

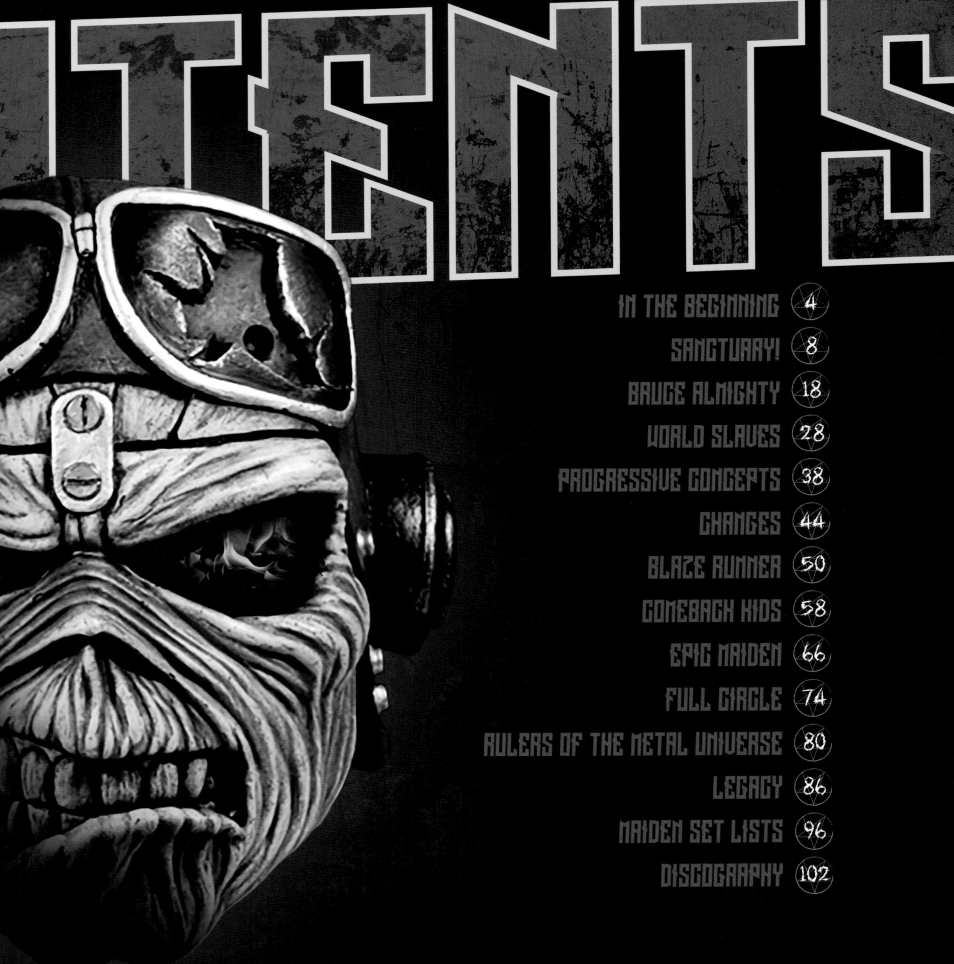

'I was a late starter'

Steve Harris

reat Britain, Christmas Day, 1975. . . Her Majesty's annual festive message was broadcast from the Buckingham Palace Gardens, Morecambe and Wise's Christmas Show saw ratings of a record-breaking 28 million, and Queen's Bohemian Rhapsody topped the charts. Meanwhile in Leytonstone, east London, a 19-year-old draughtsman and former West Ham United apprentice by the name of Stephen Percy Harris, formed a heavy rock band he promptly christened Iron Maiden, after a medieval instrument of torture he had seen in the 1939 film, The Man in the Iron Mask.

Steve, as he was known, had been a wannabe musician for two years. He loved Genesis, Pink Floyd, Yes and Jethro Tull — the big progressive rock bands of the 1970s — while also being into heavy rock bands Led Zeppelin, UFO and Deep Purple. Inspired by Led Zep's John Bonham and the Who's Keith Moon, Steve originally wanted to be a drummer but opted for the bass guitar when his east London home proved to be too small to house a kit. Having learned a few chords on an acoustic guitar, he bought a copy of a Fender Tele bass for £40 and taught himself how to play.

'*I didn't take up playing bass until I was 17,*' he recalls. '*I was a late starter.*'

After 10 months of honing his craft and learning his instrument, Harris formed his first band, Influence. They played Who covers and came second in a local talent contest before changing their name to Gypsy's Kiss, rhyming slang for piss. They disbanded shortly afterwards. In February 1974 Harris auditioned to play bass in a combo called Smiler, led by twin brothers Tony and Mick Clee.

'*I was 18 and the twin brothers were 26 and I remember thinking how old they were,*' he says. '*I just wanted the experience of playing live with good musicians and actually seeing how a band works. That's what I was able to do with Smiler because they were already gigging around the circuit.*'

The band's set mainly consisted of Wishbone Ash, Savoy Brown, ZZ Top, Free and Montrose numbers. Harris contributed two original songs Burning Ambition and Innocent Exile but Smiler were not smiling.

'*It didn't go down well because it was so far from where they wanted to be — they were a Blues Band,*' said Harris. '*So that was when I decided the only way to go was to start my own band.*'

In addition to Harris, the first line-up of the new-born Iron Maiden included singer Paul Day, guitarists Dave Sullivan and Terry Rance, and drummer Ron Matthews. After months of rehearsals, the band made their debut at St. Nicks Hall in Poplar on 1 May 1976. It was not a success. According to Harris, vocalist Day lacked '*energy or charisma on stage*'. He was replaced by Dennis Wilcock, a Kiss fanatic who used make-up and fake blood during live performances.

Wilcock would prove to be a footnote in the Maiden story but it's thanks to him that his then-friend, guitarist Dave Murray, joined the band's line-up.

Born David Michael Murray in north London on December 23 1956, Dave had fallen in love with the electric guitar on hearing Jimi Hendrix's Voodoo Child for the first time, aged 15.

'*Everything changed, just like that,*' he was to later recall. '*Getting into rock music wasn't like a gradual process for me. I heard Voodoo Child on the radio and thought, "Bloody hell! What is THAT?" And I started buying albums, thinking about getting into the big time, wondering what that would be like.*'

Murray took up the guitar. At 16, he formed his first band and played for a number of local bands before successfully auditioning for Iron Maiden in 1976. His arrival caused problems with existing guitarists, Sullivan and Rance, who felt threatened and undermined. But in Murray, Harris recognised a musical soul mate.

'*When the others made it plain that it was either them or Dave Murray, there was no choice. There was no way I was gonna let Dave go,*' he reveals. '*Not only was he a nice bloke, he was just the best guitarist I'd ever worked with. It was when Dave joined that I began to have real faith in the band.*'

In May 1977, Harris hired guitarist Bob Sawyer to play alongside Murray but he was soon sacked for embarrassing the band on stage by pretending to play guitar with his teeth. There was further tension when Wilcock and Murray argued — with the vocalist somehow managing to convince Harris to fire Murray in addition to drummer, Ron Matthews. A new line-up was put together including Terry Wapram on guitar, Tony Moore on keyboards, and drummer

Barry Purkis, later known as '*Thunderstick*'. But this combo lasted for just one performance. Harris fired Purkis and replaced him with Doug Sampson, his former Smiler bandmate. At the same time, Moore was asked to leave as Harris decided that keyboards did not suit the band's sound. A few months later, Dennis Wilcock decided to leave Iron Maiden to form his own band and Dave Murray was immediately reinstated. Wapram, wishing to be the band's sole guitarist, disapproved and so was promptly given his marching orders.

Harris, Murray, and Sampson spent the summer and autumn of 1978 rehearsing while they searched for a singer to complete the band's new line-up. A chance meeting at the Red Lion pub in Harris' native Leytonstone in 1978 evolved into a successful audition for a cocky, charismatic 20-year-old named Paul Di'Anno. Born Paul Andrews in Essex in May 1958, he was an interesting choice. Far more into punk rock than heavy rock, he'd never even sung in a band before.

'*He told me he had no experience whatsoever but that he really wanted to sing,*' Harris recalls. '*He came down to rehearsals and we played a few Purple, Led Zep and Black Sabbath covers. Then we started playing our own songs and it worked out really well. There's sort of a quality in Paul's voice, a raspiness, that just gave it this great edge. I became really hopeful when Paul Di'Anno joined the band.*'

Undeniably Di'Anno brought something special to the band, enabling Maiden to combine edgy vocals, galloping heavy rock bass rhythms and scorching hard-core riffs. The new look Maiden started gigging in pubs around east London while also holding down day jobs. This enabled them to record their own record. The band chose to record at Spaceward Studios, Cambridge.

after hearing a demo tape recorded there by former vocalist Dennis Wilcock's band, V1. Although more expensive than recording in London, they decided it would be worth it.

'*Doing it on the cheap was a false economy,*' says Steve. '*We knew we'd only probably get one go at it, and we wanted it to sound the best we could.*'

The band booked an off-off peak session at the studio on New Year's Eve 1978. It cost them £200 and they recorded four songs — Prowler, Invasion, Strange World and Iron Maiden.

'*We didn't know what to expect, going into the studio for the first time,*' Harris reveals. '*We just hoped the engineer was gonna be good enough to record us. We went in there with a naïve attitude and, as it happens, it was pretty good. The songs were very together already — very tight because we were doing them live all the time. We knew exactly what we needed to do. It was just a question of whether we could record it all in time. But I think we did most of them in the first take.*'

Following this single session on New Year's Eve, Maiden were due to return a few weeks later to remix and re-record some parts but simply could not afford the extra cost. In early 1979, Harris and Murray presented a copy of the unfinished demo to DJ Neal Kay, then running the Bandwagon Soundhouse heavy metal club in Kingsbury, north west London. Impressed with the recording, Kay began to play the tape and eventually Prowler reached No. 1 in the Soundhouse charts, which were published in Sounds music magazine. Then the tape reached Rod Smallwood, music agent and former manager of Steve Harley's Cockney Rebel. . .

'*I thought it was very, very good and I called Steve Harris,*' recalls the Huddersfield born Smallwood. '*I fixed up a couple of gigs for them — one of which was at the Swan in Hammersmith.*'

This gig hardly went to plan. Shortly before Maiden were due on stage, Di'Anno was arrested for possessing a knife.

'*Steve came up to me and said, "Paul has been arrested. What should we do?",*' Smallwood reminisces. '*About 30 kids had come down from the East End so he said — Maiden ethos, really — "We've got to play". I said, "Can you sing?" He said, "Not really." I said, "Can you try? Do you know the words to the*

songs?" He said, "I wrote them all!".'

Smallwood remembers being impressed by the way Harris and guitarist, Murray, soldiered on.

'*Harris was right — he couldn't sing — but I've never seen anything like it. It was quite special,*' he says. '*They were awesome. Not fashionable but I didn't care about that. I knew I wanted to work with them.*'

The aim was to secure a recording deal. EMI were immediately interested but in autumn 1979, while waiting to sign the deal, the band released the demo on their own label, Rock Hard Records. Entitled The Soundhouse Tapes after Kay's club, Steve Harris explains that they decided to release the EP, '*because everywhere we'd go we'd do really well at the gigs, and then afterwards there'd be all these fans asking where they could buy one of our records and when we told 'em there weren't any yet, they couldn't believe it. They'd seen the charts in Sounds and a lot of 'em just assumed we must already have a record deal of some kind, but we didn't. Not then. So then, they'd be, like, "Well, where can we get a copy of the tape?" And I think that's when we really got the idea of putting the Spaceward demo out as an actual record.*'

Deciding to release the EP as a memento for fans, the group only printed 5,000 copies, 3,000 of which were sold by mail order in the first week. The EP was so successful that, according to Rod Smallwood, many fans asked for the record at their local record stores that it reached the point where HMV and Virgin tried to order 20,000 copies each.

'*We could have really cashed in at that point,*' he says. '*It was our record, not EMI's, and we could have made enough to clear our debts, if we'd wanted to — maybe got it in the charts, even. But there was just no way. It really was something special for the true die-hard Maiden fans, and we'd already made that quite clear. If we'd changed our minds, just to get our hands on a bit of cash, it would have been selling out the kids who'd gone to all the trouble to send in for one of the original 5,000 copies. We thought, "No, we'll wait until we can do it properly with EMI".*'

They didn't have long to wait. Two months after their first headline gig at the legendary Marquee Club, the band signed with EMI records in December 1979. Finally they could give up the day jobs.

IRON MAIDEN REHEARSAL ROOM 1979

IN THE BEGINNING

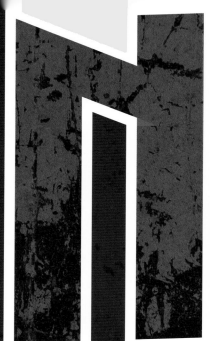

SANCT

'I reckon we're the only real New Wave HM band – we're an HM band with punk attitudes'

Paul Di'Anno

O nce signed with EMI, Maiden asked Dave Murray's childhood friend, Adrian Smith of Urchin, to join the band as second guitarist. Committed to his own band, Smith declined and Remus Down Boulevard guitarist Dennis Stratton was hired in his place. When Doug Sampson exited due to health issues, a new drummer was also required. At Stratton's suggestion, ex Samson drummer Clive Burr took Sampson's place.

Iron Maiden's first album appearance was on the Metal for Muthas compilation. Released on February 15 1980, it included early versions of the Harris-penned songs Sanctuary and Wrathchild. The release was followed by a tour, featuring several other bands coming under the New Wave of British Heavy Metal banner — a phrase invented by Sound Editor Alan Lewis.

Maiden went into Kingsway Studios, west London to record their first album, Iron Maiden, in January 1980. According to Steve Harris, the recording took just 13 days but the band weren't happy with producer Will Malone.

'I think the songs on it are really strong — it's like a "Best of" the four years before if you like — but I didn't like the production,' said Harris. 'Will didn't seem that

However Maiden fans loved the disc's aggressive, raw sound. In addition to the title track, the album included other early favourites Running Free, Sanctuary, Transylvania and Phantom of the Opera. When Iron Maiden was released in the UK in April 1980, it debuted at an astounding number four in the album charts.

'We knew that it was selling quite well and that it would get into the charts but we never expected it to enter at such a high position,' says Harris. 'The single Running Free also charted well at number 33. We thought that the album would enter the top 20 or 30 so to go in at number four was incredible. It went Gold soon after, firstly in Japan, but the UK followed on shortly afterwards, and it did amazingly well worldwide.'

Maiden made history when they appeared on legendary British TV show 'Top of the Pops' playing live.

'We told EMI we would never do TOTP unless we did it live,' says Rod Smallwood. 'After all, we were a metal band, not a pop outfit. Running Free came out and we were asked on. Well, nobody since The Who in 1974 had done it live, but we said,

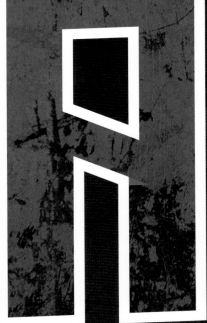

The band embarked on a headline tour of the UK, before opening for Kiss on their 1980 Unmasked Tour's European leg. This was a revelation to the Maiden boys.

'*It was a real eye-opener,*' says Dave Murray. '*We got on well with Kiss and learned a lot from them — the way they combined music with the theatrical element. If wondered if we could do the same with Maiden.*'

They had, in effect, already started. It was with the release of Iron Maiden — and the tours that followed — that the band's iconic mascot, Eddie, became known to a wider audience. The very first version of the monster had been a mask made by an art student who was friends with Dave '*Lights*' Beasley, then in charge of lighting and pyrotechnics for the live shows. According to Beasley, the original mask was a papier-mâché mould of his own face, which was then used in the band's backdrop, consisting of lights and the band's logo. At the end of their live set, during the Iron Maiden song, a fish tank pump was used to squirt fake blood out of the mask's mouth, which usually covered then-drummer Doug Sampson. After this initial incarnation, Beasley constructed a larger mask from fiberglass, equipped with flashing eyes and the ability to release red smoke from its mouth. Steve Harris states that the name '*Eddie*' comes from the fact that said mask was referred to as '*The Head*', which sounded like '*The 'Ead*' in their London accents. While according to guitarist Dave Murray the name was inspired by an old joke.

'*A wife had a baby, but it was born with only a head and no body. "Don't worry,"* says the doctor. "Bring him back in five years and we'll probably have a body for him". So, five years go by, and there's Eddie the 'Ead, as his parents have called

him, sitting on the mantelpiece, when in walks his dad. "Son," he says, "today's a very special day. It's your fifth birthday, and we've got a very special surprise for you". "Oh no," says Eddie. 'Not another fucking hat!".'*

Once Iron Maiden had secured the contract with EMI, Rod Smallwood decided the band, who despite their extrovert presence on stage were actually all rather shy, needed, '*that one figure who utterly stamped his presence and image on the band in a way that was obvious enough to make a good album cover.*' Smallwood set up a meeting with artist Derek Riggs who went on to create Eddie. Smallwood then decided the character would feature in the band's subsequent concerts and artwork. Eddie's debut appearance was on the cover of single Running Free in which his face was covered by shadow to protect his identity before the release of the band's first album. From this point on, Eddie became like the sixth member of Maiden.

August 1980 saw Maiden appearing, to much acclaim, at the Reading Festival. Shortly afterwards this success, Harris asked Stratton for a word.

'*Steve said the band didn't feel it was working out,*' Stratton later revealed. '*They were concerned that I listened to artists like George Benson and the Eagles.*'

This sounds like an excuse but it wasn't.

'*He was trying to do some writing which would have been fine if it had been the right stuff but he seemed to want to pull us in a 10 CC type direction,*' says Harris. '*That wasn't where any of us wanted to go. It became a problem and was

L-R: Clive Burr, Dave Murray, Steve Harris, Dennis Stratton, Paul DiAnno group shot, walking through park.

10

a shame. Dennis is a nice bloke and a great guitarist. Musical differences really were the reason he had to leave.'

Enter Adrian Smith — Dave Murray's childhood pal and the guitarist the band had originally wanted to recruit. Adrian was at a low ebb when he happened to run into Steve and Dave, and they again asked him to join Maiden. This time he didn't hesitate. Becoming a member of the band changed his life almost immediately as they continued to tour to the end of the year, building a reputation as a top flight live act.

'It was all quite new to me because I had never properly toured before,' says Smith. *'I'd played clubs and pubs in England, playing to from a couple of hundred people to a man and his dog. In the band I was in before Maiden, I was going to gigs on the bus with my guitar and a plastic bag with my wah pedal in it. To go from that to earning a wage every week, having a tour bus and playing in front of two to three thousand people. . . it was a huge novelty.'*

In February 1981, Iron Maiden released their second studio album, Killers. Containing many tracks written prior to their debut release, only two new songs were written for this record — Prodigal Son and Murders in the Rue Morgue, the title of the latter lifted from the Edgar Allen Poe short story of the same name. This time producer Martin Birch, who had famously worked with Deep Purple, Black Sabbath, Wishbone Ash and Whitesnake, was hired.

'Meeting Martin Birch for the first time was kind of nervy, because he was this big, respected producer,' Harris recalls. *'But we got on great with him. . . I'd always*

wanted to work with Martin as a producer. He's got a great feeling about sound and, just by listening to a band, he knows immediately what sound they should have without de-naturing the music.'

Killers was followed by the band's first world tour, which included their debut performance in the United States, opening for Judas Priest at the Aladdin Casino in Las Vegas.

'Touring the States, playing to 50,000 seater stadiums was an incredible experience,' recalls Murray.

For Harris, it came close to Beatlemania.

'Everywhere we travelled there were loads of screaming girls. I mean it was unbelievable. . . just screaming! Guys as well would run down the street and start banging on the windows. It was ridiculous.'

But not every member of Maiden was loving it. Paul Di'Anno was increasingly unhappy. He hadn't felt particularly connected to the Killers album to begin with.

'It wasn't quite there for me,' he was to later say. *'And, to be frank, at that age I wasn't handling things as well as the other guys who were older than me, One minute I was a kid off the street and the next I was expected to handle things like they were sliced bread. I started drinking and I must've done half of Peru up my nose. I was just going for it non-stop, 24 hours a day, every day. . . I screwed up. The band had commitments piling up that went on for months, years, and I just couldn't see my way to the end of it. I knew I'd never last the whole tour. It was too*

 Paul Di'Anno and Steve Harris performing live onstage 1980

much. I wasn't happy, both with the album, the touring or myself and I really didn't want to be there.'

The band members and management weren't happy with Di'Anno, either.

'We knew that we couldn't carry on with Paul,' says Harris. 'When Ron Smallwood first got involved with the band, he asked me if there were any potential problems that might crop up in the future and I said, "I've got to be honest. There may be a problem with Paul, because sometimes his attitude is a bit weird".'

During the Killers tour, Smallwood warned Rod Di'Anno about his attitude and behaviour.

'Paul started to get a bit into the whole "lifestyle" aspect of being a rock star. And I was like, "Well you better fucking control it, I'm gonna be watching you." I knew the only thing that could fuck up Maiden was Maiden themselves. But Paul was so over-the- top. He started having vocal problems, he smoked like a chimney, he drank brandy, did coke and speed, and he was missing gigs.'

Smallwood and Harris let him go in early autumn 1981. Dianno already knew the game was up.

'When you're fucked up on drugs and alcohol you turn into a complete prick,' he said. 'But I did feel relief when I played that last gig.'

This took place at Odd Fellows Mansion in Copenhagen, Denmark on September 10 1981. Future Metallica drummer Lars Ulrich was among those in the audience to see Di'Anno take his final bow. But Steve Harris had already been searching for a new singer, weeks before Di'Anno was shown the door. Former Back Street Crawler frontman Terry Slesser was auditioned behind Di'Anno's back, but his voice didn't gel with Maiden's more technical material. Harris then turned his attention to the flashy, flamboyantly dressed frontman with Maiden's NWOBHM peers Samson. Worksop-born Bruce Dickinson, aka Bruce Bruce. . .

✪ Paul Di'Anno, Clive Burr (on drums) and Steve Harris performing live onstage on Killers World Tour

IRON MAIDEN BOOK OF SOULS

Paul Di'Anno of Iron Maiden performs at Pointe East during their Killer
World Tour, Lynwood, Illinois, June 26, 1981

BRUCE D

'I stood at the back watching and thought, "Christ, this is a great band. Imagine what I could do if I was singing with that band"!'

Bruce Dickinson on seeing Iron Maiden for the first time.

Ron Smallwood didn't like Bruce Bruce.

Smallwood and Harris went to Reading Festival in 1981 in order to check out Bruce, gigging there with Samson.

'I hadn't even met him but I didn't really like him. I thought Bruce Bruce was a stupid name, I thought the white thing he used to wear on stage looked really naff, and also Samson had messed about with Maiden before I got involved — I do bear grudges.', However Steve Harris was set on him.

'Ron may not have been keen but I thought Bruce was really good, even though I'd never been much into Samson. I thought, "Yeah, the bloke's got a really good voice, and he knows how to work a crowd". I thought he sounded a bit like Deep Purple's Ian Gillan, actually. When the shit really hit the fan with Paul, he was one of the first people I thought of.'

Born August 7 1958 in in Worksop, Nottinghamshire, Bruce Dickinson began his musical career fronting small pub bands in the 1970s while attending school in Sheffield and then university in London. In 1979, he joined Maiden's NWOBHM stablemates, Samson.

'We effectively grew up together, musically, because I was in Samson, and all the bands gigged together,' says Dickinson. 'Maiden already had this momentum about them. It was like standing in front of a truck. They had that energy even before they got the record deal.'

'At Reading Festival Rod Smallwood offered me the chance of an audition — he didn't offer me the job,' Bruce recalls. 'But I had an unfeasible amount of balls and said, "Well, alright. First of all, if I do the audition, I'm going to get the job, so you need to figure out whether or not you want me on-board, because I don't want to be unless I can be a pain in the ass and have some opinions. I'm not going to be like the old guy. I'm going to have disagreements with Steve, because I've got some ideas about how I want to change things around. So, if you don't want that, you'd better tell me now". I thought it was probably best to go in there with all guns blazing. We turned up to the rehearsal room and let rip. Steve picked up the phone and said, "Could we get him into a studio today?" They were still doing gigs with Paul. The atmosphere was a bit down. When they came back from Sweden, we popped in the studio, recorded three songs and that was it. That was "job done". We all went out and got very drunk that night.'

Dickinson was officially unveiled as Iron Maiden's new frontman on stage at the Palasport arena in Bologna, Italy on October 26 1981. Following a nerve-racking UK debut for the frontman at the Rainbow theatre in London the following month, the band decamped to east London

 Iron Maiden new Singer Bruce Dickinson

to write their third album. With studio time booked at Battery Studios in north west London in December, the clock was ticking and Steve Harris in particular was feeling the heat.

'*There was a lot of pressure. Not only did we have a new singer, we had no material. The first album was like a "Best of"- the songs we'd been playing during the first four years of the band. The second album was mainly early stuff as well. When we got to the third album we had nothing. We had to write from scratch but pressure helps to make you come up with the goods.*'

It did that all right. Maiden's third album, The Number of the Beast, again produced by Martin Birch, was released in Britain in spring 1982 and by the time it was released across the pond four months later, the band were a force to be reckoned with throughout the world.

'*I had the same feeling on The Number of The Beast as when we did the Deep Purple album, Machine Head,*' said Birch. '*It was the same kind of atmosphere, the same kind of feeling — really exciting and special. I remember saying to them, "This is gonna be a big, big album. This is gonna transform your career". It just had all the magical ingredients — feel, ideas, energy, execution.*'

The album featured song writing credits from Adrian Smith and Clive Burr in addition to Steve Harris. Due to contractual obligations with Samson, Dickinson was not able to contribute in a song writing capacity.

'*I still had a legal sword of Damocles hanging over my head from the Samson contract which meant that I wasn't allowed to actually write, which was extremely frustrating, but still, the atmosphere was great,*' he recalls. '*Martin was like a guru to me, and everyone in Maiden at the time*

Iron Maiden's Bruce Dickinson jokes about

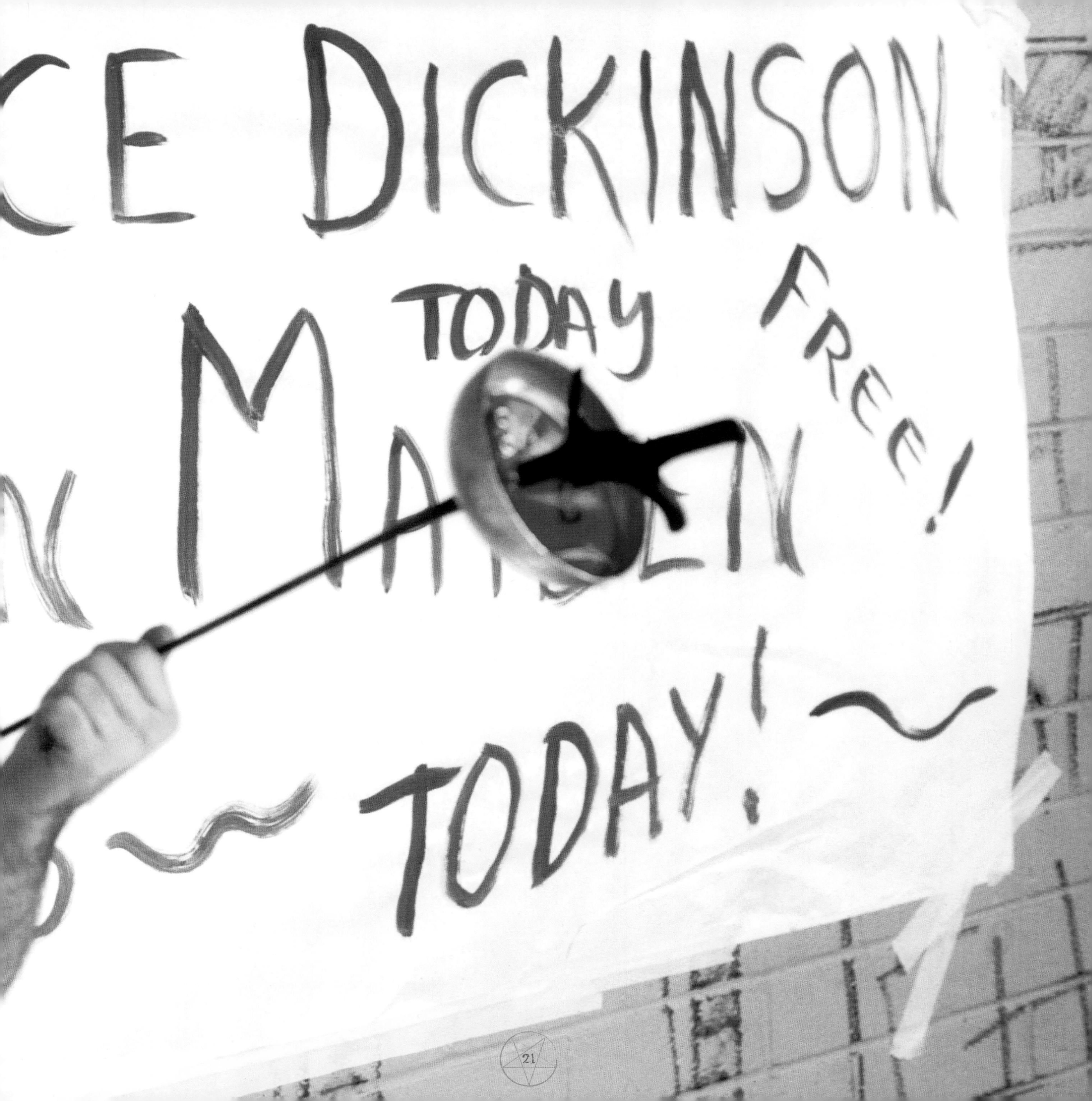
CE DICKINSON
TODAY
FREE!
TODAY!

The whole thing was just a lads' night out. We had a bloody great time.'

The first teaser for Maiden's third album was the galloping, Wild West-themed single, Run to The Hills. Released on February 2 1982, it became Maiden's first Top 10 single, entering the UK chart at Number Seven. Appearances on Top of The Pops and anarchic Saturday morning children's TV show, Tiswas followed, both considerably raising the band's profile. The exposure paid off — released on March 29, The Number of The Beast debuted in the UK album chart at Number One.

'*We were on tour in Winterthur, Switzerland when we got the news about the album,*' Dickinson remembers. '*We got a telegram on the Sunday morning going: "Your album is number one!". And we went: "Fantastic!". But at the time, we were pushing a 30-seater coach in order to jump start it, because the driver had let the battery go flat!*'

The Beast on The Road tour kicked off on February 25 1982 at Queensway Hall in Dunstable. It ran for 10 months, racking up a total of 182 shows across the globe. It was while Maiden were on the road that the first tensions between no-nonsense, working class bandleader Harris and his cocky, public school-educated new singer began to surface.

'*Steve and myself always used to clash,*' says Dickinson. '*I think he wanted to fire me after the first month of The Number of The Beast tour.*'

There was definite '*argy-bargy*' on stage and while Dickinson may have been exaggerating, Harrison definitely felt his territory was under threat.

'*At first, I thought I was imagining it,*' he says. '*But there were nights on stage during the early part of that tour when Bruce used to, like, try and jostle me on stage. It was all done in fun. . . only you could tell it was a bit more than that sometimes.*'

As vocalist, Dickinson felt that he, not the bass player, should be centre stage.

'*Steve was right up front in the middle,*' he recalls. '*And when I was watching them from the front I was like: "Hmm, I don't like the look of that, that's wrong.*

 Maiden performs at the Holiday Star Theater during their Beast on the Road Tour, Merrillville, Indiana, May 25 1982

The singer should be standing there". So, the first thing I did was move my little monitors into the middle, which got in his way. I'd be singing along, getting into the groove, and I'd feel this thump, and he'd be there, elbowing me out of the way.'

Harris admits it was an ego thing.

'*It did make me wonder if he was right for the band. I don't know if he thought he had to sort of stamp out his territory or whatever, but he didn't need to.*'

Dickinson disagreed

'*We were young and chucked into this huge shit-storm of success and we dealt with it in different ways. To a certain extent you make a Faustian deal when you join a successful band. There is a price that gets exacted upon you, and there's very little you can do about that except hope to come out the other end of it right-side up.*'

On May 11 1982 Maiden arrived in the US for more than 100 shows that would take them through to October. But in the southern states, the album's title track sparked protests from religious groups.

'*They wanted to believe all that rubbish about us being Satanists,*' said a bemused Steve Harris. '*It was ridiculous.*'

However, it brought the kind of publicity money couldn't buy. At the end of the five-month stint, The Number of The Beast had broken into the Billboard Top 40, and Iron Maiden were the hottest new metal band on the planet. The official tour bus — once Rod '*Smallwallet'*, as he was known, allowed them to have one — became party central.

'*That bus became the subject of all manner of shenanigans,*' says Dickinson. '*The experience of that first US tour was like taking a very powerful drug every night. A bunch of 24-year-olds from England let loose in America, pre-Aids, with endless supplies of drink and party material and willing young girls. . . I remember being pissed, crawling on my hands and knees down a hotel corridor, looking for bread rolls from the room service trays because I was so hungry. I caught a glimpse of myself in a mirror looking like a feral critter and I thought, "What a state you're in. Look at you!". I thought I'd better sort this out, because I could already see that 10-month world tours were going to be my life for the foreseeable future.*'

From left, Adrian Smith, Steve Harris, Bruce Dickinson, Nicko McBrain and Dave Murray in an hotel room before a show at the Holiday Star Theater during their Beast on the Road tour

24

The shows were getting bigger and bigger, with tours and albums planned months and years in advance

'*I like to make a plan and stick to it*,' says Rod Smallwood. '*We'd look ahead to what we wanted to do, how long we wanted to tour. The band lived extremely modestly on tour — we put the money back into the tours and the band.*'

1982 had been a whirlwind, ground-breaking year for Maiden but for one of their number the end of the road was nigh. That December, drummer Clive Burr played his last gig with Maiden. There are two versions of why this came to be. It's said the charming, talented Burr was indulging rather too much in the kind of rock n'roll lifestyle that had seen off Di'Anno. He was, allegedly, regularly on stage with a nightmare hangover — supposedly spending most of one gig throwing up into a bucket at the side of his drum kit. Burr's playing was starting to suffer — something Harris would just not tolerate.

'*We had problems with Clive Burr on tour and gave him three months to sort himself out*,' says Harris. '*He didn't.*'

Burr, who passed away in 2013, always maintained that he drank and partied no harder than any of the others and that he was unceremoniously booted out during a particularly vulnerable time in his life — shortly after his father's sudden death in 1982. This was mid-tour but with the apparent blessing of his bandmates, the drummer flew back to the UK to help his family cope with the bereavement. Maiden continued the tour with Nicko McBrain, who had previously drummed with '*Streetwalkers*' and the French band '*Trust*'.

'*I knew Nicko*' said Burr. '*He loved the band, he loved being part of it all — and the rest of the band liked him. When I returned to the US a fortnight later, I could tell something wasn't right, there was a meeting and I was told to leave. I was too upset to feel angry about it. I guess they had their reasons. There was a grieving period — I grieved for my dad and I grieved for my band — and then I brushed myself down and got on with it.*'

Burr's permanent replacement?

Bruce Dickinson performs at the Alpine Valley Music Theater during their World Piece Tour, East Troy, Wisconsin, August 6, 1983

BRUCE ALMIGHTY

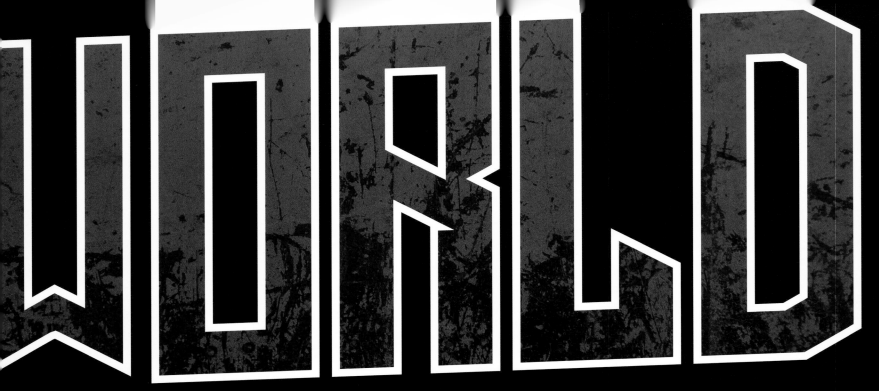

WORLD

'Nicko's arrival brought a massive charge of electricity into the band'
Adrian Smith

Larger-than-life Michael Henry 'Nicko' McBrain was a perfect fit for Maiden. He was 'one of us'.

'He was actually born about a mile and a half from me,' explained Steve Harris. 'He's giving us a different dimension. It's tougher, his timing is perfect and he hits it real hard. He's a total rock drummer.'

January 1983 saw the band decamp to a deserted hotel on Jersey in the Channel Islands to write material for their fourth album.

'There was a 24-hour bar and all the gear was set up 24 hours a day,' Dickinson recalls. 'You could wander in wearing your jim-jams, pick up a guitar and start playing, then someone else would come in, hear what you'd done and you'd start working together.'

Six weeks in and Maiden had enough material to record what would be Piece of Mind at the Compass Point Studios in the Bahamas, with producer Martin Birch once again at the controls.

Nicko, especially, was determined that it should be a success.

'It was my first album with the band and I raised my game,' he recalls. 'I was playing with one of the best rock bassists of all time, who was also a composer. It wasn't enough to just play along and I didn't want to let anyone down.'

There was no chance of that. After the success of The Number of the Beast album and tour, Maiden were flying. They were a band playing at full steam and had plenty more energy to burn.

'We were on a high and you can hear that mood on the album,' says Harris. 'Most of all though, it was just the songs. Between us, I thought we'd really come up with the goods.'

In addition to galloping bass lines, blaring harmonised guitars, epic vocals and a thundering drum sound, the lyrics on Piece of Mind contained many literary references. Harris based the lyrics of Trooper, his song about the soldier fighting in the Crimea War in 1854, on the Alfred Lord Tennyson poem, The Charge of the Light Brigade. He wrote To Tame a Land after reading Frank Herbert's, Dune. Where Eagles Dare was partially written about 1968 Brian G Hutton film, and Still

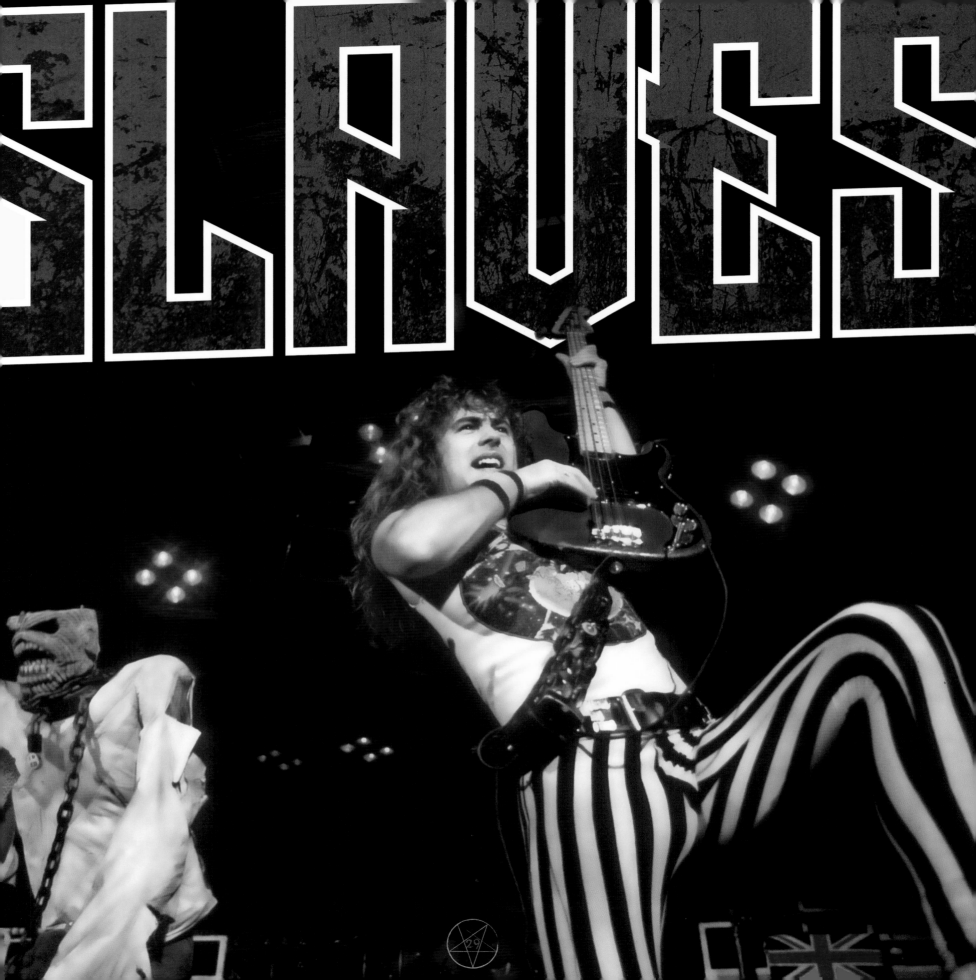

Dave Murray, Bruce Dickinson, and Eddie at the Alpine Valley
Music Theater during their World Piece Tour, East Troy, Wisconsin,
August 6, 1983

Life was inspired by a short story by Ramsey Campbell called, The Inhabitant of the Lake. Dickinson's Revelations was inspired by occultist Aleister Crowley while his and Adrian Smith's Flight of Icarus was loosely based on the ancient Greek myth of Icarus who was imprisoned with his father Daedalus in the palace of Knossos on Crete.

Dickinson and Harris had a stand-up row while recording The Flight of Icarus. It was a matter of timing.

'*He wanted to play the whole thing much faster,*' says Dickinson. '*I stood nose-to-nose with him and he reluctantly caved in and let me dictate the timing. "This is nothing to do with getting it on the radio, is it?" he demanded. ' "Oh no. God forbid. Of course not",' I lied. We did it the way I wanted and it was a top 10 radio hit.*'

Released in May 1983, the album reached number three in the UK while peaking at 14 on the US Billboard album chart. Iron Maiden supported the album with the World Piece Tour, which launched in Europe in late April 1983, crossing into North America that summer and ending in December. Lasting eight months, it was short by their standards.

After a break for Christmas and New Year, the first part of 1984 followed the same routine of the previous year with the band holing up in an out-of-season Channel Islands hotel to write material for their fifth album before jetting off to Compass Point, the Bahamas and Martin Birch.

Once again, the vibe was good. So good, in fact, that the band felt – and looked – like they were on holiday.

'*You'd get up in the morning, have a swim, spend some time by the pool,*' Dave Murray remembers, '*then you wander into the studio in the afternoon.*'

For Bruce, as the singer, there was a lot of waiting around as vocals were recorded last.

'*And waiting and waiting,*' he says. '*Along the beach from the studios was a bar called "The Traveller's Rest". It was like something out of an Earnest Hemingway novel. The banana daiquiris were of such quality that they rendered you both potent and impotent at the same time.*'

Backstage at the Alpine Valley Music Theater during their World Piece Tour, East Troy, Wisconsin, August 6, 1983, from left, Dave Murray, Steve Harris, Bruce Dickinson, Nicko McBrain, and Adrian Smith

32

Powerslave, as the album would be called, reflected Harris' prog rock roots. His Rime of the Ancient Mariner, a retelling of the Samuel Taylor Cole's epic poem, lasted almost 14 minutes. The eight-track disc also included single releases Two Minutes to Midnight and Aces High. There was a confidence and sense of continuity about Maiden that hadn't been apparent before — perhaps due to the fact that this was the first time the same line-up had completed a second album.

With Eddie depicted as a ghoulish Pharoah on the cover, the subsequent World Slavery tour took on an Egyptian theme.

'What Powerslave really did was give us the gift of Pharoah Eddie and the magnificence of the Powerslave stage set,' says Bruce Dickinson. 'We had a walk-on Eddie mummy plus a giant mummy that rose from the back of the set in a stunning finale. The theatricality was sensational. For The Rime of the Ancient Mariner we turned the same stage set into an old galleon. This was old-school painted backdrops, trompe-l'oeil effects and props. Proper theatre rather than insubstantial gimmicks. It was theatre of the mind. It was the best show that Maiden had ever put on — just the right combination of epic stuff but not too overblown. It wasn't so hide-bound by the sort of technology, loads of hydraulics and inflatable things that occurred later, all of which had the possibility for Spinal Tap-type fuck-ups on a regular basis. Virtually everything on the World Slavery Tour, apart from the lights, was done Musical Hall style — it was all boxes and ropes and two blokes pulling levers. It was so simple, you could set it up in small theatres or big arenas and it would always look fantastic.'

As Steve said, 'It could have been totally cheesy. 'Cos you think of Egypt and the pyramids and, really, how do you portray that without looking like Hawkwind? But the set was really good, it looked fantastic, and it was probably the best stage show we ever did.'

Dubbed The World Slavery Tour, this was Maiden's largest tour to date, consisting of 193 shows in 28 countries over 13 months, playing to an estimated 3,500,000 people in all. Beginning in Poland, which was at the time still behind the Iron Curtain, the band then toured North America twice before heading to Brazil where they co-headlined with Queen at the Rock in Rio festival. It was extremely successful tour but Maiden were mentally and physically exhausted by the time it ended in July 1985.

'It was the best tour we ever did and it was the worst,' says Dickinson. 'It nearly finished us off for good. I never thought it was going to end.'

 Dave Murray and Steve Harris perform at the Alpine Valley Music Theater, World Piece Tour, East Troy, Wisconsin, August 6, 1983

Adrian Smith agreed. '*These days, when bands take on 13 month world tours, they build-in gaps for recuperation. But there were no breaks on that tour, no real gaps, just a day off here and there… You're gone for a year and your whole life goes out the window, basically. As for keeping long-term relationships going — whether it's with friends or lovers, or whoever — I mean, forget it! I know it goes with the territory, but it was tough. By the end, you don't know how to act properly any more, you don't know who you are or what you're supposed to be doing. I remember I went to see my parents when I got home and I knocked on the wrong door. Honestly!*'

Rod Smallwood was working his boys for all they were worth.

'*The thing you've got to remember is Rod is an ex-agent,*' Harris revealed, '*and I don't mean a secret agent! He doesn't like to see an empty diary. But that tour was a bit like getting your darts out and throwing them at the board and that's it, that's where you're going next, sort of thing. As a manager, he wanted to keep things really boiling. But we just told him in the end, "Look, we can't carry on like this. We're gonna be all right till the end of the tour, but if we carry on another, say, three or four months, then who knows what's gonna happen". I thought it would be the last straw, basically.* '*Cos Bruce was really in a bad way by then. He sort of turned into a hermit after it was over. . .*'

Dickinson was so badly affected, he seriously considered leaving.

'*I don't just mean leaving Iron Maiden, I mean quitting music altogether,*' he said. '*I really felt like I was pretty much basket-case material by the end of that tour, and I did not want to feel that way. I just thought, nothing is worth feeling like this. I'd begun to feel like I was a piece of machinery, like I was part of the lighting rig. I was in no mood for any more backstage politics or solitary confinement in tour buses. I thought there were other things that I could do that earned much less*

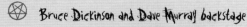 *Bruce Dickinson and Dave Murray backstage*

money but would give me the same or greater level of satisfaction. I did quite seriously think about becoming a full-time fencing coach.'

Even mild-mannered, laid-back Dave Murray had had enough.

'*The tour bus resembled a padded cell,*' he recalls. '*We'd been on it so long, it felt like the walls were closing in. The tour started to take its toll on the band, there were chinks in the armour.*'

Soon after the World Slavery toured ended, Rod Smallwood released Maiden's first full-length live album, Life After Death, recorded during the band's four shows at London's Hammersmith Odeon in October 1984 and four shows at Long Beach Arena in Long Beach, California in March 1985. A video entitled Behind the Iron Curtain documented the band's first shows in Poland, Hungary, and Yugoslavia in August 1984 — the first rock act to take a full stage show into the Eastern Bloc. Life After Death has gone on to become one of the most acclaimed heavy metal recordings of all time. Smallwood expected Maiden to tour the album but the band demanded six months off so it was scrapped, although they were granted only fourth months off rather than the six they had wanted.

When Maiden re-covened in early 1986 to write and record their sixth studio album, change was in the air. Not in terms of the line-up but with regards to the direction the band would now go in. Smith, Murray and Harris had spent their time off experimenting with new equipment while Dickinson had absorbed himself with his growing passion for fencing. Harris' prog rock influences were becoming more apparent but it seemed as though Dickinson wished to travel in a different direction. . .

PROGRESSIV

'I felt we had to come up with our Physical Graffiti or Led Zeppelin IV'

Bruce Dickinson

It was a hardly a meeting of minds when Maiden convened after four months apart. Dickinson was clearly at odds with the rest of the band.

't's not good to be in a minority of one in a five-piece band,' he said. 'Powerslave, for me, felt like the natural rounding off of Piece of Mind and Number of the Beast, that whole era. I remember listening back to it and I thought, "Ummm . . . I don't know how much more we can do of records that sound in this kind of vein". It felt we had to come up with our Physical Graffiti or whatever. Our Stairway to Heaven. Something really ground-breaking. I felt that we had to get it onto another level or we'd stagnate and just drift away. So, I went off into "acoustic world" and I wanted to do almost like an unplugged record for the next Iron Maiden album. I thought we might change radically just for the hell of it.'

He thought wrong. Dickinson wrote several acoustic songs for their next album but all were rejected by Harris and the rest of the band.

'I thought he'd lost the plot,' Harris admitted.

It fell to producer Martin Birch to break the news to Dickinson that his compositions were surplus to requirements.

'Martin took me to one side and quietly put me out of my misery,' he says. 'He told me my little acoustic numbers were not the stuff that was required. It was all pretty straightforward, and if you are crushed, better to get it over with and move on.

thought, "Why don't you just be the singer and let everyone else get on with it?" We went to Jersey again to write the next album. I did not write any of the songs so I went off to Europe to enter some fencing competitions.'

The rest of the band 'got on with it' by using guitar synthesisers on an album for the first time, marking a change in sound. The record also contained a number of songs written solely by Adrian Smith, including singles Wasted Years and Stranger in a Strange Land — this title taken from a cult novel by American author Robert Heinlein. Both songs reflected the themes of space and time, along with Harris-penned Caught Somewhere in Time and Déjà Vu. This conceptualising was accidental rather than deliberate, however.

'We certainly never went in there and said, "Right let's write a load of songs on the subject of time",' said Harris.

This was Maiden's first studio album that was released more than a year later than the previous one, the band insisting that they have more time, 'to get it right without hurrying for a change,' comments Harris. Although sounding different, it still featured galloping bass lines, soaring vocals and their signature two guitar attack. It was also one of their most expensive records to date, with the bass and drums recorded in the Bahamas, the guitars and vocals in Amsterdam and the

As with previous albums, the cover of Somewhere in Time was created by the band's then-regular artist, Derek Riggs. A cyborg-enhanced Eddie exists in a futuristic, '*Blade Runneresque*' environment. Also — again as with previous releases — images on the cover contain all manner of hidden messages and references to the band's past. For instance, the street sign on the corner where Eddie is standing reads Acacia (partially obscured), a reference to the song 22 Acacia Avenue from The Number of the Beast. Below the Acacia sign is a poster of Eddie from the first album with graffiti reading '*Eddie lives*' written on it. Torn posters were also featured on the Santuary and Women in Uniform singles. An Eye of Horus neon sign is at the top of a building, a reference to the song Powerslave from the album of the same name. To the right of Eddie's left leg there is a rubbish bin attached to a lamppost, identical to the one seen on the cover of the first Maiden album. The haloed black cat from the back cover of live album Live After Death is on the pavement behind Eddie.

Somewhere on Tour kicked off on September 1986 in Belgrade and finished in Osaka on May 21 1987. The band performed across the globe, taking in the US, Europe and Japan, and lasted 253 days, during which the band performed 151 shows. To replicate the album's arrangements live, Steve Harris's techie, Michael Kenney, played keyboards throughout — as he would on subsequent tours.

While Somewhere in Time was not a concept album, the next one most definitely was. The idea of the Seventh Son of the Seventh Son came to bassist Steve Harris after he read Orson Scott Card's book, The Seventh Son.

'*It was our seventh studio album and I didn't have a title for it or any ideas at all,*' says Harris. '*Then I read the story of the seventh son, this mystical figure that was supposed to have all these paranormal gifts, like second sight and what have you, and it was more, at first, that it was just a good title for the seventh album, you know? But then I rang Bruce and started talking about it and the idea just grew.*' After his songwriting contributions were rejected from Somewhere in Time, Dickinson felt his role within the band had diminished and he'd become '*just the singer*'. But his enthusiasm returned when Harris explained the concept to him.

'*I thought, "What a great idea! Brilliant!" And, of course, I was really chuffed, too, because he'd actually rung me to talk about it and ask me if I had any songs that might fit that sort of theme. I was like, 'Well, no, but give me a minute and I'll see what I can do." It's a classic story of good versus evil, only with no guarantees whatsoever that it's the good guys who eventually come through. Nothing and*

nobody comes out of this story unscathed. Which is everyone's story, really, isn't it? None of us get through our lives smelling of roses everywhere we go — everything is a constant battle to try and stay sane, to cut through all the bullshit that gets in our way. To find some sort of meaning, some pattern. At the same time, there's more to it than that. It's quite a mythical tale, and in trying to tell it we really allowed our imaginations to run free. It's a Heavy Metal Dark Side of the Moon.'

In addition to Dickinson's return to writing, the album was also notable for its number of co-written pieces, with five of the eight tracks being collaborative efforts. According to Harris, this was probably because they, '*spent more time checking up on each other to see what everybody else was up to, just to make sure the story fitted properly and went somewhere*'.

To make sure each song fit with the record's concept, the band drew up a basic outline for the story, which Harris states, '*didn't make the actual writing any easier ... I probably took longer over the writing I've done on this album than any I've done before. But the stuff we all started coming up with, once we'd agreed that we were definitely going for a fully-fledged "concept" album, really startled me. It was so much better than anything we'd done in ages.*'

Stylistically, this album developed the sounds first heard on Someone in Time, although on SSOASS the synth effects were created by keyboards rather than bass or guitar synthesisers. According to Dickinson, the band decided not to hire a keyboard player, with the parts being, '*mainly one-finger stuff from Adrian, Steve, the engineer or whoever had a finger free at the time.*'

Harris was delighted with the album, although it did not sell particularly well in the US.

'*I thought it was the best album we did since Piece of Mind,*' he said. '*I loved it because it was more progressive – I thought the keyboards really fitted in brilliantly – cause that's the influences I grew up with. I was so pissed off with the Americans, because they didn't really seem to accept it. Everyone said afterwards that it was a European-sounding album. I'm not so sure about that. What's a European-sounding album? To me, it's just a Maiden-sounding album.*'
So, incorporating heavy-weight themes such as reincarnation, the afterlife, mysticism, psychic phenomenon, and prophetic visions, SSOASS was recorded

Steve Harris and Adrian Smith performing live onstage on Somewhere On Tour tour

at Musicland Studios Munich with Martin Birch during the second half of 1987 and into early '88. To promote the album, the band hosted an evening of media interviews at the mighty Castle Schnellenberg in Germany prior to the record's release, before performing at a small number of 'secret' club shows, under the name 'Charlotte and the Harlots'.

In May 1988, Maiden set out on a yet another world tour, which saw them perform to more than two million people worldwide over seven months. That August, the band headlined the Monsters of Rock Festival at Donington Park for the first time, in front of 107,000 people. Though Maiden's set would go down as one of the finest to ever grace the Donington Park stage, post-show they would also learn of a tragedy that occurred earlier in the day. During the Guns n' Roses set, two fans were killed in a crowd surge. The tour concluded with several headline shows in the UK during November and December 1988, with the concerts at the NECS Arena in Birmingham recorded for a live video, entitled Maiden England. Throughout the tour, Harris' bass technician, Michael Kenney, once again provided live keyboards. During the song Seventh Son of a Seventh Son he performed on a forklift truck wearing a black cape and mask, under the alias of 'The Count'.

Maiden were on a high. The album was a critical and commercial smash, the tour had been a sell-out. But where to from here?

'How are we going to top this?' pondered Harris. 'Fucked if we know!'

Typically, Dickinson was rather more prosaic.

'If Number of The Beast brought heavy metal properly into the 1980s, which I actually believe it did, then with Seventh Son I think we've shown the way for heavy metal in the 1990s.'

But despite these lofty words, there were rumblings of disquiet amongst the band. After SSOASS, the band took an extended break — their first ever. Dickinson wrote and recorded his first solo album, Tattooed Millionaire, with ex Gillan guitarist Janick Gers. Adrian Smith also embarked on his first solo work Silver and Gold with new project ASAP, although he also felt in need of time out in order to catch his breath.

'We went from 1980 with the first album,' he was to recall. 'I came on board with the second and from then on, our feet never touched the ground.'

Within weeks of the band coming back to record their eighth album in spring 1990, one of their number had gone…

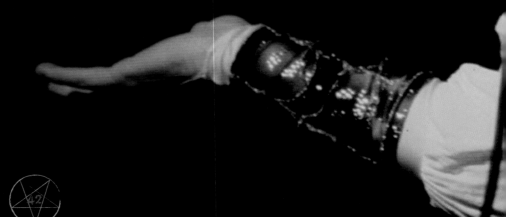

 Bruce Dickenson on stage

CHANGES

'Adrian seemed really negative about a lot of things. He just didn't seem to have the passion anymore'

Steve Harris

After a year off, Maiden reconvened at Harris' Essex mansion in January 1990 to develop their first album of the new decade. The plan was to take more time writing than they'd done in the past before recording the new album at London's Battery Studios in April. Smith was pleased, feeling that more time for writing would be beneficial to the band's development. But the joint output of Harris and Dickinson surpassed expectations and, so far as the bassist and vocalist were concerned, no extra time was required.

'When we got together for a writing session one day we ended up putting together Tailgunner, Run Silent Run Deep and Holy Smoke all in one day,' revealed Harris.

Smith, however, was slow in starting, beginning to put together just one song, Hooks in You. He felt further ostracised when Harris and Dickinson announced they wanted the band to go back to basics — back to a street-level sound in order to make a kind of anti-Seventh Son album. Smith was not happy about this development.

'The vibe was, "Let's go back and make a really raw-sounding album like Killers and I didn't want to do that,' he later said. *'I thought we were heading in the right direction with the last two albums. I thought we needed to keep going forward.'*

ditch the original plan of writing for three months in Essex before recording in London in the spring. The new idea was to immediately call in producer Martin Birch and get a mobile recording unit to tape the band in their rehearsal room. Smith was devastated by the change of plans, later stating that he'd been, *'completely thrown by the idea.'*

During pre-production, it soon became clear that key members were at odds. A meeting was called, and Smith asked to voice his grievances. He said he was still happy to contribute to Maiden but was very unhappy that the new recording plan left him little chance to actually do so. The bottom line was that he disagreed with the musical direction in which Maiden were heading. When Harris insisted that nothing less than 200% commitment to the band was acceptable, Smith felt he had no choice but to leave.

'He wasn't fired but he didn't quit entirely willingly,' said Dickinson. *'He sort-of agreed to leave.'*

Enter Janick Gers. Harris thought the Tattooed Millionaire guitarist might be just the musician person Maiden needed — *'Good guitar player … Great onstage … Good bloke.'* With no time to lose, Dickinson called Gers and asked him to learn The Trooper, Iron Maiden, The Prisoner and Children Of

'*I got a phone call one afternoon from Bruce,*' Gers recalls. '*He said, "Would you learn some Maiden numbers?" The first thing I said was, "No" because we'd agreed we wouldn't do any Maiden numbers.*'

Dickinson explained that Maiden were in fact hoping to replace Adrian Smith and the prospective Maiden guitarist turned white as a sheet. Gers auditioned the next day, suggesting that they start by blasting through The Trooper. It was a done deal right away, as Gers recalls: '*The whole thing just took off. When we finished, I was shaking with the adrenaline, and I remember Bruce saying, "Shit! That sounded incredible!".*'

Recording commenced and was completed in about three weeks. Gers worked in a very different way from his predecessor, as Harris explained: '*Recording with Janick is interesting. You have to get him in one or two takes, otherwise it just isn't happening for him, that's how he is.*'

The first Maiden record of the new decade would be titled No Prayer For The Dying and was released on October 1 1990. Two months earlier, the band had embarked on the year-long No Prayer on the Road tour which would play smaller venues and last exactly a year. They scored their first UK number one single, Bring Your Daughter…To The Slaughter on Christmas Eve 1990. Harris took this as a sign that Maiden's change of direction had been the right way to go.

'*It just made me feel excited again,*' he said. '*Like it really was all worthwhile, like a vindication that we must be doing something right. Having Janick in the band gave everybody a much-needed kick up the arse, too, because, being new, he was so enthusiastic about everything. I think it made us all open our eyes a bit and look at things in a new way.*'

In late 1991, Maiden returned to Harris' Barnyard Studio in Essex to make their ninth studio album. There were problems from the get go.

'*There were big limitations on that studio,*' Dickinson was to say. '*Fear Of The Dark was recorded in Steve's studio because he wanted it to be. He'd bought it and he'd paid for it and the band were gonna pay him back for using his studio.*'

On a happier note, Janick Gers was proving he could write as well with Harris as he could with Dickinson, showing a knack for working smoothly with both. Tracks like Be Quick Or Be Dead and Wasting Love only came about because Gers provided a new source of inspiration for an increasingly restless Dickinson. Fear of the Dark was released in May 1992, and, in time-honoured tradition, Maiden set off on the road — although playing in noticeably smaller venues across the US. The highlight of the tour was headlining at the Donington Monsters Of Rock in August '92.

In 1992, Dickinson also started work on a second solo album. He divided his time between touring with Iron Maiden and recording his own material. But by the end of the year, he decided that his solo efforts were not coming together.

New material was ditched and a period of soul-searching followed for the ambitious singer. Dickinson felt like he was on autopilot, not challenging either himself or his audience. He was frustrated, '*trying to conform to the established Maiden routine*' and was '*bored and desperately looking for other things to do.*' He went to Los Angeles to work with producer Keith Olsen.

While Dickinson was exploring new avenues with his solo material, Harris was producing and mixing the new Maiden Live project. Martin Birch had retired, leaving Harris in command. This was completely at odds with Dickinson's need for experimentation. In March 1993, as Harris rolled out his producer debut with A Real Live One while preparing to back out on the road, Dickinson decided he was leaving. His concerns seemed to be about himself and artistic relevance to the world around him

'*My problem was to establish where I belonged in modern rock music, if indeed I belonged in it at all,*' he later said. '*I was having my little artistic dark night of the soul. I realized I had no idea how to be creative outside of the framework of Iron Maiden, and it terrified me. I was thinking, "I am in an institution, and I will die in this institution if I don't do something about it, what can I do?" I had to figure out whether or not actually I belonged in the universe as a singer anymore. I began to feel that somewhere there was something else outside of Maiden that I was missing. You'd imagine that for such a potentially life changing decision I would have made a plan. But whether from plain naivety or just plain enthusiasm I hadn't.*'

It was a shell-shocked Ron Smallwood who broke the news to Dickinson's equally shell-shocked band mates. The vocalist had agreed to serve out a term of notice, however. He would complete the Real Live Tour and drop out of the band in the summer of 1993. This turned out to be something of a stretch for all concerned. Towards the end of the tour Dickinson admitted that going on stage felt like '*a*

  Bruce Dickinson performing live onstage 1990

morgue' at times. Allegations flew that Dickinson did not perform to the best of his ability. Harris and McBrain swore that he only gave his best at high profile gigs, and key members of the crew agreed. Dickinson didn't exactly deny it.

'*I would never expect Steve to understand that it was difficult for me to go on stage, emotionally difficult, because it's never emotionally difficult for Steve to go on stage,*' Dickinson said. '*So, I thought what I'll do is if I really feel like running around like a maniac I will, but if I don't I'll just go on and sing my bollocks off.*'

This wasn't good enough and Mc Brain, for one, had had enough.

'*Good fucking riddance!*' he expleted. '*I can't wait to get to the end of this tour and find a new singer. In my heart of hearts, I don't want to be doing this. I want us to find a new singer and do a new album. We ain't dead yet.*'

Harris did his best to play down anger but failed to hide his own sense of disappointment and betrayal, saying, '*Personally, I think he's maybe made a mistake, because I can't see why he couldn't do both his solo thing and Maiden.*'

Harris was used to putting a brave face on events but Dickinson's departure had come at a particularly bad time. His marriage to teenage sweetheart Lorraine, the mother of his four children, had recently ended in divorce and he was at his lowest ebb. To such an extent that the Maiden Chief considered retirement when Dickinson left the band.

'*I spoke to Davey on the phone and I suppose, at that point, I did have a doubt as to whether to carry on or not,*' he said. '*I thought, "I just don't have the strength at the moment".*'

As Maiden came close to ending, it was the softly-spoken Murray who would prove to be the saviour, providing the spark of leadership the band so desperately needed.

'*We were all really down, Steve especially, and we were even talking about packing it in,*' Murray recalls. '*We were all sitting around talking. It was probably the first real long, serious talk the four of us had had together in ages. I suddenly just got fed up talking about it and went, "Look, why the fuck should we give up just 'cause he is? Bollocks to him. Why should he stop us playing?" I hadn't really thought about it. It just came out.*'

This turned the mood around. Maiden emerged from that talk with a sense of purpose and fighting spirit. Harris said later that Murray, '*gave me the strength to believe we shouldn't give up. In the end, the strength came from Davey.*'

That strength would be put to use in finding a new singer. Maiden were looking for an X Factor.

Bruce Dickinson, with Steve Harris and Janick Gers performing live onstage at Wembley Arena

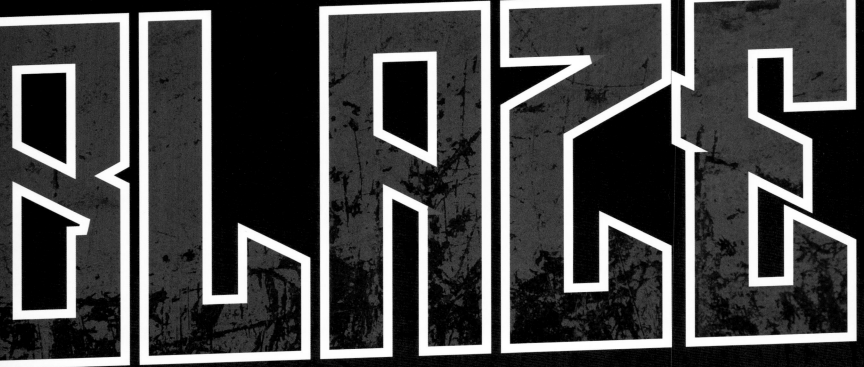

BLAZE

'It was a once in a lifetime opportunity'

Blaze Bayley

Born Bayley Alexander Cooke in Birmingham, England, on May 29 1963, '*Blaze*' Bayley was fronting Midlands' metal band, Wolfsbane, when Maiden got in contact and asked him to audition. Although he knew the band — Wolfsbane having supported Maiden in 1990 — Bayley didn't think for a moment that he would get the gig.

'*I really didn't think I would get the job because my voice is so different to Bruce Dickinson's,*' Bayley explained in 2007. '*He's much more of a technical singer and I'm much more of a blood n'guts one. I'm more about the emotion and the passion of the song. I realised auditioning for them was a once-in-a-lifetime opportunity but when they chose me, I was very, very surprised that they had chosen somebody with a very different voice. But Steve Harris heard something in my voice that he wanted to work with. He wanted to try a different sound.*'

Harris delivered the good news just before Christmas 1994. Bayley immediately told his girlfriend Debbie, then his dad, then he bought a crate of Guinness to celebrate. Telling the other members of Wolfsbane was tough.

'*Because it all happened so quick,*' he says, '*I had to tell them on the phone. It was hard. Very sad. We'd been so close.*'

Bruce Dickinson, now attempting to forge a solo career, was surprised at the identity of his replacement.

'*I said, "Has anybody given any thought to where he's going to go with the old stuff? Has anyone given any thought to how he is going to manage it? Not just singing, but how are you going to deal with the fan reaction?" Because I was surprised it was Blaze. I was delighted for Blaze, but there was a whole bunch of other really good singers out there. I thought, "Wow, they could have picked somebody with a voice that could do what my voice did". But they picked Blaze. Obviously, they picked somebody different, but that came with its own set of challenges. I just wondered whether anybody in the management was really giving anybody any serious words of truth on how hard this could be.*'

Recording Maiden's next album X Factor certainly had difficulties. Not only were the band working with a new vocalist, they also had to get used to a new producer now that Martin Birch had retired. Nigel Green, a onetime assistant of Birch's, stepped in behind the mixing desk of Harris' Barnyard Studios.

'*We wanted to make it sound very 1990s, very modern-sounding but still with the identity of Iron Maiden,*' said Dave Murray.

 Blaze Bayley

However, the prevailing tone of X Factor was doom and gloom with Harris penning a series of autobiographical numbers such as Judgement of Heaven and Blood on the World's Hands that reflected his depressed state of mind following the break-up of his marriage. Man on the Edge, written by Bayley and Gers, was the only upbeat track and it was this that was chosen to be the first single off the album. '*That was,*' Bayley recalled, '*a dream come true for me.*'

Completed in August 1995 and released two months later, X Factor proved not to have the X Factor. The fans didn't take to Bayley's vocals plus such was the strength of Dickinson's fan base, many simply weren't interested in the band without him at the helm. As a result, the album peaked at Number Eight in the UK, their lowest chart position since Killers 14 years before. It fared even worse in the US where it failed to crack the Top 100.

The critics were similarly unimpressed. '*All Music*' gave the album two stars out of five, stating that it was, '*suffering from a lack of powerful riffs and tightly written songs, The X Factor is a lacklustre, latter-day album from Iron Maiden. Although the band doesn't sound particularly bad on the record, they don't sound inspired and there's a noticeable lack of energy to the performances which makes the lack of imagination all the more apparent.*'

Meanwhile Chris Watts from Kerrang didn't mince his words when he wrote that '*X Factor*' was a '*comedy record*'. Harris was so incensed at this remark, he stormed into the magazine's office wanting to have it out with Watts who was fortunately absent that day.

'*I was really wound up,*' Harris recalled afterwards. '*I'd just spent a year of my life working silly hours doing this album and some wanker completely dismissed it in one sentence.*'

Dubbed '*The X Factour*', Maiden kicked off their next tour on September 28 1995 with a gig in Jerusalem where they had never played before. During the next year, they also journeyed to South Africa and Bulgaria for the first time in addition to touring Europe and the US. The venues were considerably smaller than on previous tours. However, it wasn't just Maiden whose popularity was in decline. With the advent of Grunge and Thrash Metal, Heavy Metal was going out of fashion. Stepping into Dickinson'*s shoes was also proving to be a challenge for Bayley. He suffered with vocal and respiratory problems during the North American leg of the tour and several dates were cancelled as a result. When the band came off the road in September 1996, Maiden released a compilation album,*

Best of the Beast. *A greatest hits* LP, it also included a new single, Virus — the lyrics of which attacked critics who had recently written off the band.

'The rats in the cellar, you know who you are. . . Or do you?' reads the penultimate line

The 1998 FIFA World Cup played a part in the title of Maiden's 11th album, Virtual XI.

'*We figure our fans are pretty much the same as we are, with pretty much the same interests, so we thought, 'It's World Cup year in '98. Let's get the football involved in the new album,*' said Harris. '*And we were already working on a computer game at that time, so we thought, "Well, let's bring that element into things, too".*'

The band went into Banyard Studios with Nigel Green in mid 1997 to work on their second album with Bayley. Although not so doom-laden as X Factor, Virtual XI again featured several longer tracks such as The Angel and the Gambler and Don't Look in the Eyes of a Stranger. The majority were written or co-written by Harris.

'*It was a more upbeat album,*' said Bayley. '*We'd survived the "X-Factour". . . we were a band. I felt we were on our way.*'

It was wishful thinking. Released in March 1998, Virtual XI peaked at number 16 in the UK and only reached 124 in the US. As with X Factor, it failed to go gold in any territory and was the poorest selling album in Maiden's 20 year history, shifting less than a million copies worldwide. It was also thoroughly panned by the critics.

'*On the surface, there's nothing terribly wrong with the record, as it delivers all the crunching riffs and demonic horror of their best records,*' read the review in All Music. '*The problem is that there's nothing memorable about the hooks, riffs, or songs, and there's little visceral energy to the music or production. As a result, it sounds lifeless to all but the most devoted fan.*' They also referred to Bayley as '*a competent but faceless vocalist.*'

Harris appeared to be as upbeat as ever, cheering himself up by helping to remaster the band's entire discography, up to and including Live at Donington.

 Dave Murray and Blaze Bayley of Iron Maiden perform on stage at Brixton Academy, on November 10th, 1995 in London

'We're not cool,' he said. 'There's other new things going on. The only time we were trendy was in '83, '84. We're not cool because we've been around for so long but I'm proud of "Virtual XI". There's no compromise as usual. We still do what we do. I'm proud of that.'

Maybe so but questions were being asked. It was a given that Metal was no longer as popular — especially in the US — but it was also apparent that Bayley had never gelled with Maiden fans, a fact that was made very clear when he was regularly booed and heckled during the US leg of the Angel and Gamblers World Tour. Again, he had trouble with his voice and some dates were cancelled when he reportedly suffered from an allergic reaction to stage props. The tour limped to a close in late '98 and in January 1999, the inevitable happened. Bayley was '*let go*' and asked to leave during a band meeting. The dismissal took place due to issues Bayley had experienced with his voice during both tours, although Janick Gers stated that this was partly the band's fault for forcing him to perform songs which were beyond his natural register.

'*It was a total shock to me,*' claimed Bayley. '*We finished in Brazil in December 1998 and in January 1999 I was fired. There I was working on lyrics and songs for a third album, which I thought, in my own foolish heart, "This is really going to turn things around". The fans are gonna go, "Now we understand why Blaze is there. This is really good". But I didn't get that chance. I was gutted by that. I think it took me about four years, really, before I kind of accepted what happened.*'

Maiden already had a replacement in mind. Having been sounded out by Ron Smallwood, it became apparent that Bruce Dickinson wasn't averse to coming back after six years as a — not altogether successful — solo artist.

Initially old adversary Steve Harris wasn't sold on the idea.

'*I wasn't really into it but then I thought, who should we get? The thing is, we know Bruce and we know what he's capable of, and you think, "Well, better the devil you know". I mean, we got on well professionally for, like, 11 years, and so. . . . after I thought about it, I didn't really have a problem with it.*'

Typically, Dickinson was rather more prosaic.

'*I had gone through my own rebirth,*' he wrote in retrospect. '*Rejoining Maiden would be restarting the music of the spheres. If the universe had been frozen for a*

Steve Harris, Janick Gers and Blaze Bayley, with Blaze Bayley singing performing live onstage at Rock City, Nottingham

few years, I felt we could walk through the walls of ice and into a world of fire and passion. Rejoining Maiden lit the blue touch paper for an incendiary future and I relished the challenge.'

Bruce, however, had a condition he wanted fulfilling before he returned. He insisted that guitarist Adrian Smith also be asked back after nine years away.

'When he left the band in 1990, I think everybody was a bit surprised at how much we missed him and certainly, I don't think anybody had realized how much the fans would miss him — big time,' said Dickinson. 'I wouldn't have rejoined Iron Maiden if he wasn't in the band. I just don't think it would have been complete without Adrian, and now, it's great having three guitarists.'

Smith's own solo career had amounted to little and he was delighted to be reunited with Maiden - if a tad confused

'It was quite complicated. I'm still not quite sure how it happened,' he said. 'It was just a kind of planets aligning — it just seemed like the right time. It's just been great for me to do it second time around. Maybe do a few things differently than the first time. I certainly appreciate it more now.'

Janick Gers, who had replaced Smith in 1990, could well have felt threatened by his predecessor's return but it seemed to be a case of the more guitarists, the merrier.

'To me, this isn't a reunion it's a step forward,' he said 'We are moving forward and there is no way that the band is just getting back together for a tour and some money. For starters, this is a new line-up and the second is that this is not just a bunch of old farts getting back together. We want to go back into the studio and make what could be the best Iron Maiden album ever made.'

But first, the new six-piece went back on the road . . .

L-R: Steve Harris, Nicko McBrain, Adrian Smith, Bruce Dickinson, Janick Gers and Dave Murray on a New York street

COMEBA

'Rejoining Iron Maiden was like slipping on your favourite pair of hiking boots'

Bruce Dickinson

The Ed Hunter Tour, running from July to October 1999, served as a kind of rehearsal and warm-up to Gers' *dream of making 'Maiden's greatest album'*. The newly reunited sextet that was now Iron Maiden immediately gelled as a unit.

According to Dickinson there was a, '*New energy and sparkle. It started the ball rolling, it started winding people up',* while for Smith the tour proved to be, '*One of the most enjoyable tours of my life — and I've done a few'*.

Dave Murray, too, was delighted to have his former band mates back by his side.

'*The chemistry within the band has increased with getting Bruce and Adrian back. The magic that was there before, I think we can recreate it again. There's a real excitement between everyone. You can really feel it and I think it's going to be great.'*

Steve Harris echoed these sentiments.

'*We could've just gone in and done an album but we thought it best to go and do some live shows first. . . Basically we wanted to go into the studio and add all the vibes, all the freshness of coming off a tour and playing together again.'*

As they had done in the past, Maiden took off to an out-of-season resort to write the next album. But in Portugal rather than the Channel Islands.

'*Steve had a house in Faro and we all decamped to holiday villas and apartments in a tourist colony to write,'* recalls Dickinson. '*So we were all living in the same place for three months with everyone knocking on each other's doors and writing individual bits. Then we all got together in one room and presented songs and that's pretty much how the record got made — with everyone writing with everyone else. In fact, because there are six guys now in the band, and five of us are writers, it's makes for a lot of variety.'*

In November 1999, Maiden started working with South African born, California-based producer Kevin '*Caveman'* Shirley at the Guillaume Tell studios in Paris. Shirley, who had previously worked with Journey, Rush and Aerosmith encouraged the band to play live in the studio for the first time.

'*One of the things I really like to do is capture a band playing live in the studio,'* disclosed Shirley. '*I suggested to them that they record Brave New World like that, and they were sceptical in the beginning, because they had always worked through overdubbing. But they ended up loving it. You get things very quickly this way and you get a real sense of whether things are happening. One of the things that's quite unique about Iron Maiden is the push-pull between the different musicians. Steve Harris really pulls the band along with his bass guitar, he's*

always a little ahead of the drums. You could go into the computer and put him right on the beat, but then you get a totally different feel that's not Iron Maiden. By recording them live I could really capture their sound.'

Shirley achieved this — and then some. Musically all three guitarists, plus Harris, were on fire, crafting a combination of volcanic riffs and catchy hooks with songs like The Wicker Man — inspired by the 1973 cult horror film of the same name. The title track — Brave New World — was written after Dickinson re-read the Aldous Huxley novel while Out of the Silent Planet was influenced by the 1956 sci-fi movie Forbidden Planet.

For Dickinson, this was Maiden at their very best. Indeed, he named it as his favourite IM album to date.

'All respect due to Piece of Mind, which is my previous favourite record and still sounds good, but this is just one level of brutality beyond that…' he said. 'The musicianship within the band is so scarily good. People don't even realize how good the players are in Maiden. That's why it's possible for us to do it. We're not sad old f--kers getting back together to go and make a few bucks. That's sad and cheesy, and not something I'm interested in.'

The new-look trinity of axemen was certainly paying off.

'If ever there was a band where three could complement the music, it is Maiden,' Dickinson added. 'There are a lot of guitar harmonies and guitar parts. The songs are long and there's a lot of space for three guitar players. The characters of the three guitarists blended very well. Jan has this completely anarchic style, which, in a sense, he can now be set free as before he had to fulfil Adrian's parts. Davey has a very distinct style. They all have.'

Released in May 2000, Brave New World peaked at number seven in the UK chart and debuted at No. 39 on the Billboard album charts. While this was a definite step-up from their previous few releases, it was not a big hit in comparison to Maiden's 1980s output.

Never one to hold back, Dickinson had something to say about this.
'I still think the band may be a little too quirky in its own way for the kind of triple-platinum type audience,' he said. 'In the '80s, we were too heavy, and all the hair

 Janick Gers performing with Eddie

bands went quintuple-platinum. We sold a million, and we did cool. Then, all of a sudden, everything's flipped around now, and now everything's really atonal, and yelling and screaming and everything, and people are wondering whether Maiden's heavy enough. We actually transcend all that bulls--t.'

Reviews for Brave New World were largely positive.

'The strongest and most self-assured outing since Seventh Son 12 years prior — proof positive that the Cockney boys could still deliver,' wrote Sounds music paper. 'The only thing louder was the collective sigh of relief from metal heads across the planet.'

Sputnik Music considered that, 'Brave New World sounds like what you would expect an Iron Maiden album to sound like. Great harmonies and melodic riffs can be found all over the album, as they always have, and unless Steve Harris loses it, always will. Bruce sounds like he never left the band, only it's 1988 not 1992.' Maiden launched the Brave New World tour on June 2 2000 — though the European leg was known as Metal 2000. Like 1986's World Slavery Tour, various incarnations of Eddie featured on stage. One was made from wicker — referencing the song The Wicker Man — and contained a posse of 'maidens', comprising the band and crew's girlfriends, catering and wardrobe girls. At the show's climax, they emerged and dragged Dickinson into the wicker tomb. The 'maidens' in Norway were rather rougher than normal with the result that the vocalist emerged with bite marks and scratches.

'It looked like I'd had an argument with a barbed wire fence,' he said.

In order to prove they were no band of 'has-beens', Maiden played six songs from the new album on the BNW tour.

'I think it is even quite brave of us to play the amount of new stuff we play,' said Harris. 'Whenever we go out on tour with a new album, we always play at least six new songs. A lot of people don't do that. They are sacred of reactions so they only play one new song. They are worried about people bitching about their new material but I think it shows a lack of confidence in their new product.'

In all, Maiden completed almost 100 gigs on this tour which were and mostly trouble-free. Apart from a show in Germany in July 2000 when Janick Gers slipped and fell off the stage. The guitarist dropped some ten feet to the venue's floor, leaving him unconscious and bleeding from his forehead. Gers also sprained his back and suffered additional bruising, and he received six stitches at a local hospital. He was ordered to rest for at least a week and as a result, Maiden has had to cancel shows in Germany, Bulgaria and Greece. Once Gers had recovered, the band took off for North America where the lacklustre tours of the Blaze years proved to be a distant memory. The Madison Square Garden concert on 5 August sold out in two hours. A whole new generation were discovering Iron Maiden.

'I noticed there was this new set of fans, young kids, coming to the shows,' said Adrian Smith. 'The first thing I noticed when I got on stage was these young kids upfront because I was expecting people of that generation who grew up with us really, basically our age. I know, having kids myself, that they're really into the artwork, the whole Eddie thing. That draws them in — the really young kids — and then they get into the music.'

As a tour finale, Maiden headlined at the world-famous Rock 'n Rio festival in Brazil on January 19 2001 in front of a 250,000-strong audience. It was the second largest crowd they'd ever played before, the largest being at the same festival 16 years before during the World Slavery Tour. The performance was recorded for CD and DVD release.

 Performing at Shoreline Amphitheater in Mountain View California. September 16th, 2000

'It was a massive live TV audience and a one chance live recording opportunity,' remembers Dickinson. *'I had myself locked in my hotel room for two days in the dark, just resting and rehearsing in my mind. When I hit the stage I felt like a greyhound being released from a trap. The heat and humidity were exausting but the adrenalin kept on coming — to the point that I thought either my heart would burst or my legs fold under me.'*

What Maiden hadn't known at the time was that there were technical issues, with just a third of the PA working as they performed. Steve Harris, in particular, found this to be problematic. Due to the PA malfunctioning on the edge of the stage, Harris said he, 'had to stay firmly within my area for the whole night, which meant that I could not interact with the crowd as much as I would have liked.

While the Rio performance was being edited and produced, Maiden took a well-earned break. Not that Steve Harris ended up having much of a rest. Although he had had been behind the band's previous two concert films, Maiden England (1989) and Donington Live (1982) Harris had decided not to edit this project himself.

'I wanted a fresh pair of eyes on Maiden,' he said. *'I was after someone else's input and direction over my style.'*

A professional company was hired but when Harris saw the first edits while producing the soundtrack with Kevin Shirley in New York, he promptly changed his mind. According to Harris, the editors had opted for several 'styling decisions' which included 'deliberate out of focus shots of the lighting rig which just horrified us.' Additionally, the crew had also lost from two cameras, meaning there were very few shots of Dave Murray and Adrian Smith. To remedy the situation, Harris reluctantly decided to undertake the editing work himself, despite being 'burnt out and ready for time off' following the tour's conclusion. To achieve the desired results, Harris had to teach himself how to use complex digital editing systems and installed all the necessary equipment in his home studio in Essex.

It was a tragedy that brought the band back together earlier than planned. In 2001, former Maiden drummer Clive Burr had announced that he'd been diagnosed with multiple sclerosis. As a result, he was deeply in debt and was in danger of losing his home. His former band mates came to his aid. From March 18-21 2002, Maiden staged a series of charity concerts at the Brixton Academy in London, with all proceeds going to the Clive Burr MS Trust Fund which the band helped to set up.

 Adrian Smith, Dave Murray, Janick Gers performing live onstage, 2001

EPIC T

'All I do is bring out the best in them'

producer Kevin Shirley

A t the end of 2002, Maiden went into the Sarm West Studio, a converted church in Notting Hill, West London which Jimi Hendrix had once called home, to record their 13th album, Dance of Death. Kevin Shirley was once again producing.

'It was great and second time around was better because we didn't have to go through all the bullshit of getting to know each other,' recalls Steve Harris. 'We knew what each other wanted. There were a lot of similarities with Martin Birch. Both have a great sense of humour. Their overall professionalism is about the same.'

For the first time, drummer Nicko McBrain had a songwriting credit, having co-written New Frontier. As a born-again Christian, the track expressed his concerns with human cloning.

'I personally believe that God created man and it is only God's right to create a human being because only He can give you a soul,' he said. 'When man attempts to make man then it's a monster in a test tube.'

 Nicko McBrain, 2003

McBrain was initially unsure about his abilities as a song writer.

'I was nervous,' he admitted. 'I had all the lyrics and melodies worked out but I took it to Adrian and we worked on bridge and chorus together. I also asked Bruce for help.'

The reaction from McBrain's bandmates was overwhelmingly positive.

'It took him 20 years so no wonder it's good,' quipped Steve Harris. 'The bottom line is that it is a great song. If it wasn't, it wouldn't be on the album.'

Dickinson plundered history for the lyrics of his epic track, Montségur, based on the fall of the Cathar stronghold of the same name in 1244.

'There is so much great stuff and so many great stories throughout history that you can make parallels with the modern day,' he said, 'particularly when history repeats itself as often as it does — that it makes for some very colourful subject matter.'

It was history again that inspired Adrian Smith to write Paschendale — about the Battle of Passchendaele which took place during the First World War. With its extended length, detailed structure and multiple tempo changes throughout, Paschendale was, as Smith described it, '*a traditional Maiden epic*'. For Dickinson, the song was a '*powerful and stirring body of music.*'

According to guitarist Janick Gers, the album's title track was inspired by the final scene of the Ingmar Bergman film, The Seventh Seal. '*At the end of the film these figures on the horizon start doing a little jig, which is the dance of death,*' he explained. Gers wrote most of the music and explained the concept to Steve Harris, who then wrote the lyrics and most of the melody.

Face in the Sand, notable for being the first and only Iron Maiden track in which McBrain uses a double bass pedal, was based on the media coverage surrounding the second Iraq War which was taking place as the album was being recorded.

'*I remember thinking about the desert sands as an image and how it moves and shifts with time,*' said Dickinson. '*Specifically, what I was thinking was that whatever empires you tend to build — whether they are British, American, Iraqi or whatever, they'll all crumble and fade away into something else. So, to my mind at least, the best thing you can hope for, if you were to leave anything behind, is just an imprint in the sand.*'

The final track, Journeyman, is Iron Maiden's first and only fully acoustic song. The song was originally recorded with electric instruments, however, as Dickinson stated that, '*after all the battering that we've given the listener over the last hour of music it just seemed right to play out with something totally unexpected and left field.*'

The ideas, it seemed, were flowing.

'*As we went through the recording process, more and more ideas started creeping in — some of which we hadn't even dealt with in rehearsals,*' remembers Dickinson. '*And some of the ideas were really nice. We'd be working on a song and it was like, "Gosh, I never quite expected that to happen".*'

Before releasing Dance of Death, Maiden went on the road on the Give Me Ed. . .till I'm Dead tour, having committed to it back in 2001. Starting in May 2003 in Spain and ending three months later in California, the band played classic songs from their back catalogue rather than newly penned tracks. Maiden's faithful following

were delighted by old favourites such as The Number of the Beast, Acacia Avenue, Bring Your Daughter to the Slaughter and Run to the Hills. They also played new track Wildest Dreams which would be the first single off Dance of Death.

'*It's sort of a cross between Number of the Beast and Run to the Hills,*' said Steve. '*I put it together in a couple of hours and then played it with Steve, and he said, "Oh, that would make a great single". And he wrote the words. It came together pretty quick.*'

It was Maiden's intention to build-up their fan base to what it had been in the 1980s.

'*In North America and to a certain degree the UK, we lost a lot of ground and it's a challenge to try and win those people back,*' said Harris. '*It would be nice to get it back where it was.*'

Released in September 2003, Dance of Death was a critical and commercial success worldwide, dancing its way into top 10 UK album chart — peaking at number two, and the Top 20 of Billboard 100. The BBC hailed it as a return to form. However, the album cover caused controversy. An amateurish, computer-generated attempt at placing Eddie in the middle of an Eyes Wide Shut-inspired fever dream, the image adorning Dance Of Death was a confusing mess including characters with comically contorted necks and limbs, scantily-clad girls and an infant awkwardly sitting on a dog that was awkwardly standing on a snake. It appears, the band decided to go with artist David Patchett's '*unfinished prototype*' rather than his completed work. Patchett subsequently demanded his name be removed from the album credits.

The Dance of Death tour, starting in October 2003 and ending in February 2004, has gone down in history as one of Maiden's greatest ever. The stage was decorated to look like a medieval castle, with two towers on either side of the runways, and featured Grim Reaper statues and a castle gate between them for the opening song. The stage floor was decorated to look like a twelve-point star, identical to the one featured in the Dance of Death artwork.

The tour was notable for its extensive use of props and other theatrics. Bruce Dickinson would begin Dance of Death from a throne on the left podium, wearing a cape and two Venetian masks. He later sported a Grim Reaper cloak. Paschendale began with battlefield sound effects reminiscent of

L-R: Dave Murray, Janick Gers, Steve Harris, Bruce Dickinson, Adrian Smith, Nicko McBrain, studio group shot

EPIC MAIDEN

the First World War, during which the road crew, dressed in military uniform, placed models of dead bodies and barbed wire around the set while Dickinson recited the first two stanzas of '*Anthem for Doomed Youth*' by World War One poet, Wilfred Owen. A giant Eddie would later appear from the back of the set during the song Iron Maiden, wearing a cloak and wielding a scythe. It also made an appearance as the Grim Reaper during The Number of the Beast.

The tour was subject to a short number of cancellations, with the band's shows in Wrocław, Rotterdam and Helsinki being postponed while Bruce Dickinson recovered from flu and laryngitis. In addition to this, the second show in New York was cut short after one audience member dropped a beer on the soundboard.

In 2005, the band announced the Eddie Rips Up the World Tour, which, tying in with their 2004 DVD entitled The History of Iron Maiden — Part 1: The Early Days, only featured material from their first four albums. As part of this celebration of their earlier years, The Number of the Beast single was re-released and went straight to No. 3 in the UK Chart. The tour included many headlining stadium and festival dates, including a performance at Ullevi Stadium in Sweden to an audience of almost 60,000. This concert was also broadcast live on satellite television all over Europe to approximately 60 million viewers.

Following this run of European shows, the band co-headlined the US festival tour, Ozzfest, with Black Sabbath. Maiden earned press coverage world wide for their final performance at the Hyundai Area in San Bernardino, California on 20 August 2005 — but not for the right reasons. Their final show was sabotaged by singer Ozzy Osbourne's family. Throughout the tour, Bruce Dickinson had reportedly made several detrimental comments about reality TV, specifically '*At Home with The Osbournes*'. He had also inferred that Ozzy and Sabbath made use of autocue during their performance, and questioned the fact that Iron Maiden had headlined several dates of the tour — due to Ozzy suffering from illness. Sharon Osbourne, Ozzy's wife and manager, took offence, placing family and friends in the crowd to sabotage Iron Maiden's performance by throwing eggs, bottle tops and lighters from the front of the audience. In addition, the PA system was shut off multiple times, cutting off power to Dickinson's microphone and the band's instruments mid-song while members of other bands were recruited to cause further disturbance, such as by running on-stage with an American flag during The Trooper. These efforts to ruin Maiden's show seemed to have been in vain, however, as the band

 Steve Harris performing live onstage, playing Fender Precision Bass

reportedly played even better as their performance was disrupted. Shortly after Iron Maiden's set, Sharon entered the stage to the unanimous boos from the crowd and stated that, while she loved Iron Maiden, Dickinson was a '*prick*'.

Following the show, Iron Maiden's manager Rod Smallwood issued a statement condemning the incident. '*In 30 years in this business. . . I have never seen anything anywhere near as disgusting and unprofessional as went on that night.*'

Recently, however, Dickinson has dismissed the incident.

'*It was a complete storm in a teacup. I grew up listening to early Sabbath with Ozzy. Ozzy and Sabbath are icons so that's that, end of story*', he's been quoted as saying. '*The fact that I don't like reality TV shows, well I'm not gonna offer an olive branch to the Kardashians either.*'

Maiden completed the tour by headlining the Reading and Leeds Festivals in late August, and the RDS Stadium in Ireland on 31 August. For the second time, the band played a charity show for The Clive Burr MS Trust Fund, which took place at the Hammersmith Apollo in London. Then in October that year, the band were inducted into the Hollywood Rock Walk on Sunset Boulevard, Los Angeles.

'*We got to put our hands in some cement and finally made an impression on America,*' quipped Bruce Dickinson. Who else. . .

Bruce Dickinson of Iron Maiden performs at Ozzfest 2005 at the Hyundai Pavilion on August 20, 2005 in San Bernandino, California

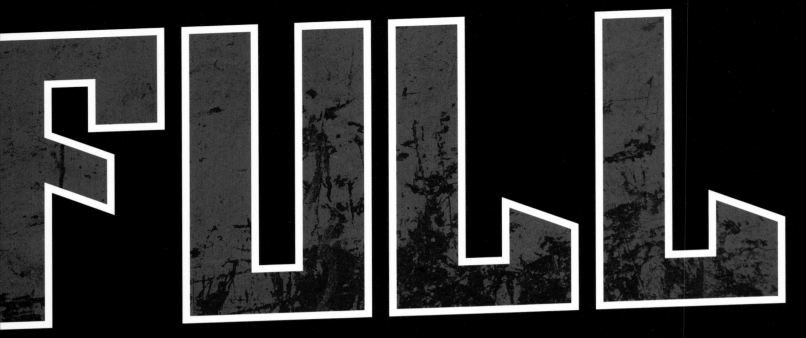

FULL

'This album is a step up in everything else we've done in my opinion'

Nico McBrain

Towards the end of 2005, Iron Maiden began work on A Matter of Life and Death, their 14th studio album, which was recorded at Sarm West with now-regular producer Kevin Shirley at the controls. In order to produce a more '*live*' sound, the album was not mastered — a decision taken by Steve Harris.

'*When you work in a digital format and you've got your mixes sounding just how you want, you don't really need a great deal of tweaking,*' he said. '*Well, we don't. When things are tweaked, they affect everything across the board. We did try different things and different frequencies and this and that. But it didn't sound any better really. Sounded different but not better. A lot of what you hear on the album are first takes.*'

The band's triumphant of guitarists came in for particular praise from Kevin Shirley.

'*Davey's playing is the best I have heard from him — fluid, melodic. . .there's no one like him. In contrast Adrian is razor sharp, blistering precise and in the mix Janick throws some madness — the stuff that's outside the box, as he's always looking for a way to be dangerous*'

The album was, according to Bruce Dickinson, a complete joy to make.

'*We rehearsed, learned each song and then by the time we got to the end of three weeks, we just managed to learn all the songs, just managed to get through every song. Then we'd sort of forgotten the first one but we had it on tape so we went straight in the studio the first day and went 'Hey let's listen to the tape. Play it. two or three times. Right start recording. And that's how we recorded the album — each song at a time. We haven't worked that fast since we did Number of the Beast and Piece of Mind in the early days. We recorded the album in three weeks and were just having a really good time, writing really good music and then, all of a sudden, we were like, "Wow! We're done!" I think it is one of the finest Maiden albums we've made and I'm really proud of it.*'

Regarding the content of A Matter of Life and Death, Harris stated, '*it's heavier than we've ever been, but also very progressive*'. Lyrically, the songs reflected their own lives rather than brave-heart tales from long ago. Brighter Than a Thousand Suns, for instance, was inspired by the atomic bomb. These Colours Don't Run was the story of a soldier in an unknown war. The Longest Day dwelled on the Second World War. . . Maiden originally intended to name the album after one of the tracks, as they had done with Number of the Beast, Seventh Son of a Seventh Son and No Prayer for the Dying, but nothing seemed quite right.

'*Sometimes a title will just leap out at you as the obvious choice,*' commented Janick Gers, '*but it didn't this time for some reason.*'

 Adrian Smith, Dave Murray, Janick Gers performing live onstage at the Hartwall Areena

74

Subsequently, the band decided on A Matter of Life and Death – reportedly one amongst several title ideas kicking around at the time.

After the embarrassment over the Dance of Death cover, American Artist Tim Bradstreet was commissioned to create the art work for A Matter of Life and Death. Best known for his work on the Hellblazer and Punisher comics, Bradstreet was a big Maiden fan who drew much influence from Derek Riggs' artwork. He described landing the commission as 'one of my wildest dreams' and portrayed Eddie as a general, leading an army of skeletons.

Released in August 2006, reviews for A Matter of Life and Death were glowing.

'The strongest Maiden album in 20 years,' hailed the Brave Words/Bloody knuckles website. 'Iron Maiden have utterly surpassed themselves,' enthused Metal Hammer, rating the album 10 out of 10. The BBC music praised the band's 'uncanny ability to write great lyrics wrapped around guitar orchestration that rock fans crave'. Sputnik Music also gave it full marks, commenting, 'A Matter of Life and Death contains everything fans want to hear; be it exciting, Maiden-style story telling; aggressive riffs; impressive solos; or melodic harmonies.' While PopMatters rated it 8 out of 10, deeming it, 'their most focused record since 1988's Seventh Son of a Seventh Son, one that eschews crowd-pleasing anthems in favour of massive, sprawling compositions.'

The album earned Maiden their first Top 10 entry in the US while it peaked at number four in the UK. It was also awarded Album of the Year at the 2006 Classic Rock and Roll Honours Awards.

The Matter of Life and Death World tour commenced in October 2006 and was something of a change of direction for the band. Instead of playing a few songs from the new album along with their classic hits, Maiden took a leap of faith, deciding to play the new album in its entirety. Only for the encore would they play a handful of old favourites.

'To the outside world, it looked like madness to play a whole album of new material,' said Dickinson at the time. 'To us, though, it was essential in order to lay down a marker with what was an increasingly young fan base. There were kids whose first IM record was Brave New World, not Number of the Beast. They were the future and they were

 Maiden pose for a group portrait at the Lokomotiv Stadium on June 4th 2007 in Sofia, Bulgaria

the people to carry the torch for the band, It was for them that we played the album. It was a gamble.'

One that failed to pay off. The fans wanted to hear Greatest Hits rather than A Matter of Life and Death. Responding to this, Maiden decided they would revert to type for the second leg of the tour, which they renamed 'A Matter of the Beast', to celebrate the 25th anniversary of the release of The Number of the Beast. This tour opened in March 2007 at the Dubai Desert Rock Festival, Maiden's first appearance in the Middle East. They then moved on to India where they played before 30,000 plus people in the grounds of the Bangalore Palace — the first Heavy Metal band to perform in the sub-continent. A number of European dates followed, including an appearance at Download Festival, their fourth headline performance at Donington Park, before approximately 80,000 people. On 24 June they ended the tour with a performance at London's Brixton Academy in aid of The Clive Burr MS Trust fund.

In 2008 to support the release of the Live After Death performance DVD and Somewhere Back in Time: The Best of 1980-89, Maiden embarked on the Somewhere Back in Time world tour. The tour was advertised as a way of bringing back the 1980s stage show and forgotten 'classics' for an audience of younger fans who hadn't been born in time to witness the original. Many of Maiden's songs had not been played live in a long time while the likes of Moonchild and Rime of the Ancient Mariner had never been played by the current line-up. The stage set was based around that of the widely celebrated World Slavery Tour of 1984—85, featuring similar pyrotechnics and the return of the giant mummified Eddie while also including a lighting rig and cyborg walk-on Eddie based from the 1986 Somewhere on Tour.

The first section, commencing in Mumbai, India on February 1 2008, consisted of 24 concerts in 13 countries in 45 days to 500,000 fans. They played their first ever concerts in Costa Rica and Colombia, and their first shows in Australia and Puerto Rico since 1992, travelling nearly 50,000 miles in the band's own chartered Boeing 757 which was specially converted to carry the band, their crew and twelve tonnes of equipment. Named 'Ed Force One', the plane was flown by Dickinson, now a fully qualified passenger jet pilot. It had been Dickinson's idea for Maiden to charter — and fly — a plane and as a PR coup it was priceless.

'Taking Ed Force One around the planet and playing to our fans in so many different countries was an incredible experience for all of us,' he said. 'I personally found that flying and performing was one of the most challenging and satisfying things I've ever done, despite the rigours and the many logistical difficulties we encountered.'

It was too good an opportunity not to record on camera. The documentary 'Iron Maiden: Flight 666', was filmed during the first part of the Somewhere Back in Time world tour between February and March 2008. Despite showing the technical aspects behind the tour, the documentary was predominantly about the group's fans, with Dickinson commenting that, 'Two-thirds of the film is not about us' and that real story of Iron Maiden was the relationship with their fans. Scenes shot in South America were particularly focused on the audiences, where, it was reported, Maiden were 'venerated like football stars'. The film was deemed a great success when it was released in early summer 2009, topping the music DVD charts in 22 countries. However not every member of the band had welcomed the opportunity to appear — warts and all — in a documentary. While Dickinson and drummer Nicko McBrain were the most comfortable with the filming, guitarist Adrian Smith took longer to adapt, and Janick Gers largely ignored the crew until the final week.

'I wasn't really happy about it,' he said. 'I don't want to be a film star. Bands should have a bit of mystery about them and I think if you go in with cameras and see how everything works, a lot of that is better left unsaid. Once you demystify it, it's not so interesting.'

The last part of the tour took place in February and March 2009, with the band, once again, using Ed Force One. The final leg included the band's first ever appearances in Peru and Ecuador, as well as their return to Venezuela and New Zealand after 17 years. The band also played another show in India (their third in the country within a span of two years) at the Rock in India festival to a crowd of 20,000. At their concert in São Paulo on 15 March, Dickinson announced on stage that it was the largest non-festival show of their career, with an overall attendance of 63,000 people. The final leg ended in Florida on April 2 after which the band took a well-earned break. Overall, over both years, the tour reportedly had an attendance of over two million people worldwide. At the 2009 BRIT Awards, Iron Maiden won the award for Best British live act. Voted for by the public, the band reportedly won by a landslide. Maiden were on a roll, reflected in a comment made by drummer Nico McBrain.

'In the mid 80s people said it was the height of our career,' he said. 'Well it was then but this is the height of our career really, because we've come full circle and now we're doing it again.'

Janick Gers performing live at the Sziget Music Festival, Budapest, Hungary on August 12, 2008

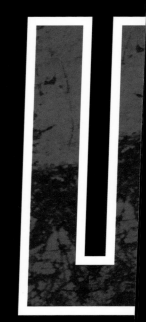

RULERS OF THE METAL U

'Maiden have never been bigger and it's all on their own terms'

the BBC

2010 saw Maiden back in the studio, recording their 15th album which would be named The Final Frontier. In a nod to the past, the band and producer Kevin Shirley flew out to the legendary Compass Point Studios in the Bahamas where they had recorded Piece of Mind in 1983.

'Recording it in the Bahamas was a little strange,' Dickinson recalls. *'It was not the place it had been in '83. Most of the charm had been replaced by American concrete. In my hotel, I could have been in Florida, Vegas or anywhere else in the USA. The studio had the same vibe and it was exactly as it had been in 1983, nothing had changed! Even down to the broken shutter in the corner ... same carpet ... everything ... It was really quite spooky. But we felt very relaxed in such a familiar and well-trodden environment and I think this shows in the playing and the atmosphere of the album.'*

Following the success of The Meaning of Life and Death, expectations for this album were high.

'There's always a bit of pressure to follow up the last album,' revealed Adrian Smith. *'In a way, it's good because it motivates you. We never get complacent — we always try our best for our own sake as much as anything else. As far as pressure for another album, we just do what we do. We've been doing it long*

enough now — we know what we're doing.'

It was a time-honoured formula. Relocate to write – Paris in this instance – then rehearse, then record. As always, they gave themselves a time-limit.

'We don't allow ourselves too long,' explained Harris. *'If you allow yourself six months to write, you'll take six months. So, we tend to put ourselves under a bit of pressure. It's not rushed — it just makes you feel a bit anxious because you know you've got to come up with good stuff. But that's always a good thing — a positive thing. A little black cloud goes away when you know you've got enough songs and you've got good material.'*

They had that all right. The Final Frontier featured some of their most ambitious and intricate work. From the delicately crafted power ballad Coming Home, the moody Mother of Mercy, heavy-rocking Alchemist through to the epic Where the Wind Blows, based on the Raymond Briggs novel about nuclear devastation, and the sci-fi inspired Satellite 15 . . . The Final Frontier. At 76 minutes long, it was their lengthiest recording to date. According to Dave Murray, TFF was a 10-track collection of *'straight-ahead, up-tempo rock songs with good groves with some*

✷ Eddie on stage at The Soundwave Music Festival at Olympic Park on 27th February 2011, in Sydney, Australia

other tracks that are kind of longer and more complex.' The album was mixed at Kevin Shirley's own studio in Malibu, California. For the producer, working with Maiden was one of the best experiences of his working life.

'I will tell you that Iron Maiden are the best band in the world to work for,' he said. 'It's a family and they are the most grounded guys I have ever met in this business. Nary a Ferrari in sight.'

The Final Frontier was released on August 16 2010 to massive worldwide acclaim. The BBC hailed it as a 'remarkable achievement from the metal titans. . . no compromises, just complexities and challenges and more moments of brilliance than perhaps even they thought they still had left in them', Classic Rock praised it as being 'densely layered and substantial', as well as 'beautifully paced and disarmingly complex' and 'a fresh take on a sound that has admirably withstood three decades of fashions and fads.' Kerrang! called it 'a record that'll still bowl you over in a decade's time' while MusicRadar stated that 'Iron Maiden have created a work full of hypnotic excitement, unconventional structure and dizzying vision...the group have succeeded beyond their wildest dreams.'

These rave reviews were reflected in sales. TFF was Maiden's greatest commercial success in their history, reaching No. 1 in twenty-eight countries worldwide. Record company EMI even felt moved to comment that they were 'very proud of their 30-year career long involvement with Iron Maiden.'

For Bruce Dickinson, this was a moment of triumph.

'The world needs Iron Maiden,' he proclaimed.

The Final Frontier tour had kicked off in June 2010, with Dickinson once again flying the band around the world in a 757 — adorned with a new 'Final Frontier'-themed coat of paint. New destinations included Singapore, Indonesia and South Korea. Over 10 months and 98 shows performed across the globe, Maiden played to in excess of two million plus fans. During the tour, the band were awarded a Grammy for best heavy metal performance. Maiden's last gig on The Final Frontier Tour was at London's O2 Arena on August 6 2011.

Once the tour ended, it was rumoured that Maiden had gone into semi-retirement and that The Final Frontier was their final album. This was happily not the case.

'No, it 'aint going to be the last record,' confirmed Nico McBrain. 'Not as far as I'm concerned. The general feeling is that if we want to make another record, we will.'

They were, however, burnt out.

'We were all feeling a little fried by the end of it,' Dickinson recalled. 'Unlike the Powerslave Tour, we acknowledged it to ourselves and I had a particularly robust evening with Ron Smallwood. There was no question, I said, of anyone walking away but if we did not manage our bodies as we got older, our bodies might just do the walking on our behalf. I made the suggestion that "little and often" was a better strategy than trying to reconquer the world every year. We would last longer and be more effective, and the world wouldn't get fed up of us being in its face every five minutes.'

Although Maiden took the latter half of 2011 and the first part of 2012 off, a number of compilation albums and DVDs were released during this time. A double disc set entitled From Fear to Eternity was released in summer 2011, covering the period from 1990-2010. Live versions with Bruce Dickinson were included in place of original recordings which featured Blaze Bayley. In March 2012, En Vivo!, footage from the Chile concert, was released worldwide on CD, LP, DVD, and Blu-ray. In addition to the concert footage, the video release included an 88-minute tour documentary, entitled Behind The Beast, containing interviews with the band and crew.

On 15 February 2012, the band announced the Maiden England World Tour 2012—14, which was based around the 1989 video of the same name. It would be, in the words of Bruce Dickinson, 'a big resumé tour – an unashamed tour with all the greatest hits'. It would also be Iron Maiden's third concert tour to take a retrospective look at a particular period in the group's history, following 2005's Eddie Rips Up the World Tour and 2008—2009's Somewhere Back in Time World Tour.

'We haven't changed arrangements or anything like that,' said Steve Harris. 'The songs still stand up as being strong as they are, so we're not changing them.'

There was a certain nostalgic excitement to revisiting some of their vintage material.

 Bruce Dickinson performing at Wacken Open-Air WOA in Wacken, Schleswig-Holstein, Germany, 5th August 2010

'*We thought it'd be fun to go back to that period in time,*' revealed Adrian Smith. '*It's just great revisiting some of the songs we haven't played for a long while. It keeps us fresh.*'

Beginning in North America in the summer of 2012, the first leg of this Maiden England World Tour would be the band's most extensive US tour, comprising 34 dates. Janick Gers confirmed that they would be pacing themselves.

'*You have to keep yourself physically fit and together,*' he explained. '*You hear a lot of bands cancelling a tour because of "nervous exhaustion" but what that means is that they've got so drunk they can't do the gig anymore. I don't drink during the day. I'm a night drinker. You look after yourself. You have to be physically fit. It's not a game. You can't be ill. You're travelling a lot, you're eating different foods and no one's going to look after you but you.*'

Following the 2012 tour of the United States and Canada, the tour continued with worldwide shows and festivals in 2013. A low point came when in March 2013, former drummer Clive Burr, passed away following complications from multiple sclerosis.

'*This is terribly sad news,*' commented Steve Harris. '*Clive was a very old friend of all of us. He was a wonderful person and an amazing drummer who made a valuable contribution to Maiden in the early days when we were starting out.*'

A highlight of the tour was performing at Download Festival on June 15 2013, marking Maiden's record-breaking fifth headline appearance at Donington Park

25 years after their first concert at the venue which they headlined in 1988 where Monsters of Rock was originally held. To commemorate this anniversary, their show began with a flypast by a Spitfire TE311 from the Battle of Britain Memorial Flight aerial display group.

'*I couldn't believe it when Rod telephoned me to tell me he had arranged for a Spitfire to open Donington — as in a real Spitfire from the Battle of Britain memorial flight,*' recalls Bruce Dickinson. '*The idea was that it would fly over the top of the stage moments before we started our intro tape for Aces High. It was a heart-stopping moment and Donington's collective jaw dropped. Grown men fought back tears. No one will forget that moment. It upstaged everything.*'

By the close of 2013, Maiden had played 46 concerts to an estimated 1.2 million fans. On December 2 2013, the band announced that the Maiden England tour would finish with a number of European shows and festivals in the summer of 2014, with the final concert taking place at Sonisphere Knebworth on 5 July. Following the Spitfire flypast which preceded their performance at Download festival the previous year, Bruce Dickinson, piloting a Fokker Dr.I, joined the Great War Display Team in a '*dogfight tribute*' in honour of the First World War's 100th anniversary.

Even by Maiden's standards, Maiden England had been a monster tour and the first since 1991, 1998 and 1988 in which The Prisoner, Afraid to Shoot Strangers and Seventh Son of a Seventh Son were played respectively. It was also notable for being the band's first tour in which Hallowed Be Thy Name — from The Number of the Beast album was not played since its release. But now, after two years on the road, it was time to go back into the studio. . .

 Bruce Dickinson, performs in Santiago, 10th October 2013

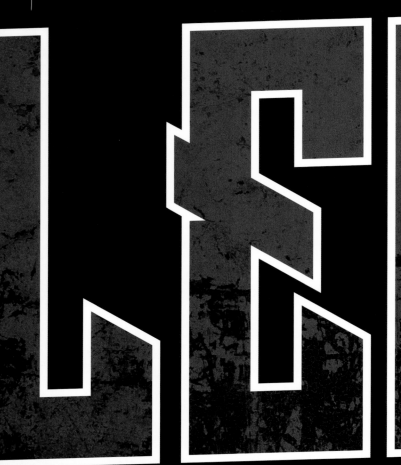

LEGAC

'Whatever "it" is, we've still got it'

Bruce Dickinson

Maiden broke with what was their time-honoured formula of writing and rehearsing completed songs before starting the recording process for their 16th album in September 2014. The aim was to give it a more live feel.

'*We went into the studio with only outlines and finished writing the songs in the studio — so we were actually learning them, rehearsing them, and putting them down all at once,*' explained Janick Gers.

This was, according to Bruce Dickinson, '*one of the best decisions we ever made.*' As was recording back at the Guillaume Tell Studios in Paris where Maiden created Brave New World in 2000. '*The studio holds special memories for all of us,*' he added. '*We were delighted to discover the same magical vibe is still alive and very much kicking there.*'

Such was the band's creative output, it was decided that this 16th studio release should be a double album — Maiden's first — with a running time of 92 minutes.

'*I love the whole feel of a double album, that warm 70s vibe,*' commented Dave Murray. '*It reminds me of when I was a teenager, buying Physical Graffiti by Led Zeppelin.*'

The double album was names Book of Souls after one of the tracks.

'*It comes from the Mayan culture in South America,*' explained Steve Harris. '*It intrigued me, in the same way that I was interested in ancient Egypt when we did Powerslave. The Mayans believed in the Underworld and were scared of losing their souls. That mystical element was the key to the title song.*'

This track became one of producer Kevin Shirley's favourites.

'*It's over 10 minutes long and begins with a mid-tempo groove,*' he commented. '*Six minutes in and it explodes into a blistering horse race of a song! Bruce's singing in the chorus has to be heard to be believed. I can't squeak as high as that guy can sing in full voice. He truly is a freak of nature.*'

 Maiden perform onstage during The Book of Souls World Tour – Shanghai concert on April 26, 2016

Other tracks included Maiden's longest-ever running track, Empire of the Clouds, lasting 18 minutes. Featuring Dickinson on piano for the first time, it was based on the 1930 R101 airship crash. Aircraft were also an inspiration for Death or Glory, another epic Dickinson composition about First World War triplanes. The vocalist named Tears of a Clown, which Steve Harris co-wrote with Smith, as his favourite track from The Book of Souls which was rumoured to be based on comedian Robin Williams' depression and subsequent suicide in 2014.

'*Steve came up with the title and it could be about Robin Williams,*' said Smith. '*It could be about Robin Williams. It's about people who hide their true feelings. It was very shocking what happened to him, but it happens to a lot of people.*'

Speed of Light was a Smith/Dickinson collaboration which was deliberately shorter than the majority of tracks on Book of Souls, harking back to 1984's Two Minutes to Midnight and Can I Play With Madness from 1988. '*We haven't done anything like that since I've been back in the band,*' said Smith. '*So that was different.*'

The band were very happy with the finished product.

'*We all brought different things to it,*' said Janick Gers. '*A really broad spectrum of musical ideas. This album dictates where we are now. We're not a band that looks backwards. I think this album proves that we're still valid — the songs are powerful and edgy. There's all types of different songs on this album and there's something for everyone — classically influenced, jazz influenced, rock and blues influenced — it's all there and is indicative of what the band's about.*'

The plan was to release Book of Souls in early 2015 but then life got in the way. In December 2014 Bruce Dickinson was diagnosed with cancer. Malignant tumours had been found on his tongue although this was not made public at the time. It later transpired that Dickinson had suspected something was seriously wrong with his health during the recording of Book of Souls.

'*I knew something was wrong in my body,*' he said. '*I felt like I was getting a cold, there were flecks of blood when I brushed my teeth and I was sweating at night. One of the glands in my neck was swollen and there was an odd*

Steve Harris performing at the Rock in Idro Festival at the Arena Parco Nord in Bologna. Bologna, Italy. 1st June 2014

smell coming from the back of my throat. I plugged the symptoms into search engines and, given my age, came up with a diagnosis of squamous cell carcinoma. This I then ignored. I had an album to do. I was singing well and was having a great time. The last thing we needed was a Google hypochrondriac.'

But his symptoms became more persistent. Once recording had finished Dickinson finally consulted a doctor. The diagnosis came shortly after and treatment commenced in January 2015. However, the illness became public knowledge only once this seven week period was over.

As the tumour was caught in the early stages, the prognosis thankfully is extremely good,' the statement on the Iron Maiden website revealed. 'Bruce's medical team fully expect him to make a complete recovery with the all clear envisaged by late May. Bruce is doing very well considering the circumstances and the whole team are very positive.'

They were right to be. The All Clear was given, as predicted, in May.

The Book of Souls was released four months later in September 2015 to

Steve Harris, Dave Murray and Janick Gers in concert at Mediolanum Forum of Assago. Assago, Italy. 22nd July 2016

largely rave reviews. It was scored 9/10 by Classic Rock, who stated, 'it's hard to think of another band of this vintage that would be capable of sounding this vital and inspired'. The Guardian also scored it 4 out of 5 and exclaimed that 'The Book of Souls is marked by an impressive rawness that scratches against the album's more grandiloquent moments'. While Kerrang labelled it, 'an album of extraordinary vision'. It reached Number One in the UK and Four in the US.

The Book of Souls World Tour Maiden had been planning was put back to early 2016 in order to allow Dickinson to fully recuperate.

'We are of course all absolutely delighted that Bruce's doctors have pronounced him free of cancer,' cited manager Rod Smallwood. 'Although Bruce is naturally eager to resume Maiden activities, it will take a while before he completely back to full strength. Because of this, the band will not be touring or playing any shows until next year. We know our fans will understand the situation and, like us, would prefer to wait until Bruce is back to his usual indefatigable levels of fitness before going out on the road.'

The Book of Souls World Tour finally kicked off in Florida on February 24 2016.

IRON MAIDEN BOOK OF SOULS

The first leg saw the band play 117 shows in 36 countries across six continents — North and South America, Asia, Australasia, Africa, and Europe, and included their first ever performances in China, El Salvador, and Lithuania. As with 2008-09's Somewhere Back in Time World Tour and 2010-11's The Final Frontier World Tour, the group travelled in a customised aeroplane, flown by Dickinson and nicknamed '*Ed Force One',* although for this tour they travelled in a Boeing 747-400 jumbo jet. Maiden completed the tour in 2017 with further European and North American shows. On 20 September 2017, The Book of Souls: Live Chapter was announced. Recorded throughout The Book of Souls World Tour, it was released on November 17 2017. In the summer of 2016, the group had launched a mobile game, Iron Maiden: Legacy of the Beast. Inspired by the game's title, the band undertook the Legacy of the Beast World Tour in 2018.

From the outset Maiden wanted this to be their most spectacular tour ever.

'*I'm focused on what's gonna constitute an amazing set list and what's gonna constitute an amazing stage show,'* said Dickinson. '*I want people to go, "Wow, you've gotta see this show". I want people to be surprised as well.'*

They were that alright — and continue to be. The Legacy of the Beast World Tour was a spectacle from the get-go. As Aces High opened the show, a 33' wide replica of a Spitfire plane, complete with propeller and flashing lights, swooped over the band. At the song's climax, the aircraft dived behind the wall of amps and crashed to the ground. Other incredible sets included the stage transforming into a church chancel, complete with stained glass windows, featuring episodes from Eddie the mascot's life, a battleground as Dickinson took on a 10-foot-tall Eddie in a duel, and a blindingly stunning display of pyrotechnics.

Swedish music festival Sweden Rock Festival 2018

Will there be a 17th Maiden studio album? Happily, so it would seem.

'*I'm pretty damn sure we will do another album,'* says Harris, '*and then all well and good, we'll go out on tour to back that up.'*

It is a time-honoured formula that has worked — and then some. Iron Maiden are considered one of the most successful heavy metal bands in history, with The Sunday Times reporting in 2017 that the band have sold over 100 million copies of their albums worldwide. They are a phenomenon that have lasted over 40 years and are regarded as one of the most influential and revered bands of all time. Like fine wine, they seem to improve with age rather than decline.

'*We are more successful now than we have ever been,'* says Dickinson. '*Everyone asks me what the secret is but there is no secret. The secret is hiding in plain sight. What you do is you take your fans then you add to them and the way you do that is by engaging with them and going out and touring. You do whatever you do with integrity and you tell the fans the truth and you do your best to deliver.'*

The last word has to go to Steve Harris.

'*Personally, I'm enjoying it more than ever, I'd say,'* he has commented. '*I think we all are. Since we had that scare with Bruce's health, everything has been even more enjoyable. Ultimately, at this point you know you've had most of your career and there's less ahead than there is behind you, but we'll definitely make more albums and we're having a great time. This is still the best job in the world.'*

LEGACY

SET LISTS

IRON MAIDEN TOUR 1980
The Ides of March
Sanctuary
Prowler
Wrathchild
Remember Tomorrow
Charlotte the Harlot
Killers
Another Life
Transylvania
Strange World
Innocent Exile
Phantom of the Opera
Iron Maiden
Running Free
Drifter
I've Got the Fire (Montrose cover)

KILLERS TOUR 1981
The Ides of March
Wrathchild
Purgatory
Sanctuary
Remember Tomorrow
Another Life
Genghis Khan
Killers
Innocent Exile
Murders in the Rue Morgue
Twilight Zone
Phantom of the Opera
Iron Maiden
Running Free
Transylvania
Drifter
Prowler
Strange World
I've Got the Fire (Montrose cover)
②② Acacia Avenue
Children of the Damned
The Prisoner
Run to the Hills

BEAST ON THE ROAD TOUR 1982
The Ides of March
Murders in the Rue Morgue
Wrathchild
Run to the Hills
Children of the Damned
The Number of the Beast
Another Life
Killers
②② Acacia Avenue
Total Eclipse
Transylvania
The Prisoner
Hallowed Be They Name
Phantom of the Opera
Iron Maiden
Sanctuary
Drifter
Running Free
Prowler

PIECE OF MIND TOUR 1983
Where Eagles Dare
Wrathchild
The Trooper
Revelations
Flight of Icarus
Die With Your Boots On
②② Acacia Avenue
The Number of the Beast
Still Life
To Tame A Land
Phantom of the Opera
Hallowed Be Thy Name
Iron Maiden
Run to the Hills
Sanctuary
Drifter
Prowler

WORLD SLAVERY TOUR 1984/5
Aces High
② Minutes to Midnight
The Trooper
Revelations
Flight of Icarus
Rime of the Ancient Mariner
Powerslave
The Number of the Beast
Hallowed Be Thy Name
Iron Maiden
Run to the Hills
Running Free
Sanctuary

SOMEWHERE ON TOUR 1986/7
Caught Somewhere in Time
② Minutes to Midnight
Sea of Madness
Children of the Damned
Stranger in a Strange Land
Wasted Years
Rime of the Ancient Mariner
Where Eagles Dare
Heaven Can Wait
Phantom of the Opera
Hallowed Be Thy Name
Iron Maiden
The Number of the Beast
Run to the Hills
Running Free
Sanctuary

97

SEVENTH TOUR OF A SEVENTH TOUR 1988

Moonchild
The Evil that Men Do
The Prisoner
Infinite Dreams
The Trooper
Can I Play With Madness?
Heaven Can Wait
Wasted Years
The Clairvoyant
Seventh Son of a Seventh Son
The Number of the Beast
Hallowed Be Thy Name
Iron Maiden
Run to the Hills
Running Free
Sanctuary

NO PRAYER ON THE ROAD 1990/91

Tailgunner
Public Enema Number One
Wrathchild
Die With Your Boots On
Hallowed Be Thy Name
②② Acacia Avenue
Holy Smoke
The Assassin
No Prayer for the Dying
Hooks In You
The Clairvoyant
② Minutes To Midnight
The Trooper
Heaven Can Wait
Iron Maiden
The Number of the Beast
Bring Your Daughter... to the Slaughter
Run to the Hills
Sanctuary

FEAR OF THE DARK TOUR 1992

Be Quick or Be Dead
The Number of the Beast
Wrathchild
From Here to Eternity
Can I Play with Madness?
Wasting Love
Tailgunner
The Evil That Men Do
Afraid to Shoot Strangers
Fear of the Dark
Bring Your Daughter... to the Slaughter
The Clairvoyant
Heaven Can Wait
Run to the Hills
② Minutes to Midnight
Iron Maiden
Hallowed Be Thy Name
The Trooper
Sanctuary
Running Free

REAL LIVE TOUR 1993

Be Quick Or Be Dead
The Number of the Beast
Prowler
Transylvannia
Remember Tomorrow
Where Eagles Dare
From Here to Eternity
Wasting Love
Bring Your Daughter...to The Slaughter
The Evil That Men Do
Afraid to Shoot Strangers
Fear of the Dark
The Clairvoyant
Heaven Can Wait
Run to the Hills
② Minutes to Midnight
Iron Maiden
Hallowed Be Thy Name
The Trooper

THE X FACTOUR 1995/6

Man on the Edge
Wrathchild
Heaven Can Wait
Lord of the Flies
Fortunes of War
Blood on the World's Hands
Afraid to Shoot Strangers
The Evil That Men Do
The Aftermath
Sign of the Cross
② Minutes to Midnight
The Edge of Darkness
Fear of the Dark
The Clairvoyant
Iron Maiden
The Number of the Beast
Hallowed Be Thy Name
The Trooper

VIRTUAL XI WORLD TOUR 1998

Futureal
The Angel and The Gambler
Man on the Edge
Lightning Strikes Twice
Heaven Can Wait
The Clansman
When Two Worlds Collide
Lord of the Flies
② Minutes to Midnight
The Educated Fool
Sign of the Cross
Hallowed be Thy Name
Afraid to Shoot Strangers
The Evil That Men Do
The Clairvoyant
Fear of the Dark
Iron Maiden
The Number of the Beast
The Trooper
Sanctuary

SET LISTS

THE ED HUNTER TOUR 1999

Aces High
Wrathchild
The Trooper
② Minutes to Midnight
The Clansman
Wasted Years
Killers
Futureal
Man on the Edge
Powerslave
Phantom of the Opera
The Evil That Men Do
Fear of the Dark
Iron Maiden
The Number of the Beast
Hallowed Be Thy Name
Run to the Hills

GIVE ME ED...TILL I'M DEAD TOUR 2003

The Number of the Beast
The Trooper
Die With Your Boots On
Revelations
Hallowed Be They Name
②② Acacia Avenue
Wildest Dreams
The Wicker Man
Brave New World
he Clansman
The Clairvoyant
Heaven Can Wait
Fear of the Dark
Iron Maiden
Bring Your Daughter...to The Slaughter
② Minutes to Midnight
Run to the Hills

EDDIE RIPS UP THE WORLD TOUR 2005

The Ides of March
Killers
The Prowler
The Trooper
Remember Tomorrow
Where Eagles Dare
Run to the Hills
Revelations
Wrathchild
Die with Your Boots On
Phantom of the Opera
The Number of the Beast
Hallowed Be Thy Name
Iron Maiden
Running Free
Drifter
Sanctuary

BRAVE NEW WORLD TOUR 2000/02

The Wicker Man
Ghost of the Navigator
Brave New World
Wrathchild
② Minutes to Midnight
Blood Brothers
Sign of the Cross
The Mercenary
The Trooper
Dream of Mirrors
The Clansmen
The Evil That Men Do
Fear of the Dark
Iron Maiden
The Number of the Beast
Hallowed Be Thy Name
Sanctuary

DANCE OF DEATH WORLD TOUR 2003/04

Wildest Dreams
Wrathchild
Can I Play With Madness?
The Trooper
Dance of Death
Rainmaker
Brave New World
Paschendale
Lord of the Flies
Hallowed Be Thy Name
Fear of the Dark
Iron Maiden
Journeyman
The Number of the Beast

A MATTER OF LIFE AND DEATH WORLD TOUR 2006/02

Different World
These Colours Don't Run
Brighter Than A Thousand Suns
Wrathchild
The Trooper
Children of the Damned
The Reincarnation of Benjamin Breeg
For the Greater Good of God
The Number of the Beast
Fear of the Dark
Run to the Hills
Iron Maiden
② Minutes to Midnight
The Evil That Men Do
Hallowed Be Thy Name

SOMEWHERE BACK IN TIME WORLD TOUR 2008/09

Aces High
② Minutes to Midnight
Revelations
The Trooper
Wasted Years
The Number of the Beast
Run to the Hills
Rime of the Ancient Mariner
Powerslave
Heaven Can Wait
Can I Play With Madness?
Fear of the Dark
Iron Maiden
Moonchild
The Clairvoyant
Hallowed Be Thy Name

MAIDEN ENGLAND WORLD TOUR 2012/14

Moonchild
Can I Play With Madness?
The Prisoner
② Minutes to Midnight
Revelations
The Trooper
The Number of the Beast
Phantom of the Opera
Run to the Hills
Wasted Years
Seventh Son of a Seventh Son
Fear of the Dark
Iron Maiden
Encore
Aces High
The Evil That Men Do
Sanctuary

LEGACY OF THE BEAST WORLD TOUR 2018/19

Aces High
Where Eagles dare
② Minutes to Midnight
The Clansman
The Trooper
Revelations
For the Greater Good of God
The Wicker Man
Sign of the Cross
Flight of Icarus
Fear of the Dark
The Number of the Beast
Iron Maiden
The Evil That Men Do
Hallowed Be Thy name
Run to the Hills

THE FINAL FRONTIER WORLD TOUR 2010/11

The Wicker Man
Ghost of the Navigator
Wrathchild
El Dorado
Dance of Death
The Reincarnation of Benjamin Breeg
These Colours Don't Run
Blood Brothers
Wildest Dreams
No More Lies
Brave New World
Fear of the Dark
Iron Maiden
The Number of the Beast
Hallowed Be Thy Name
Running Free

THE BOOK OF SOULS WORLD TOUR 2016/17

If Eternity Should Fail
Speed of Light
Children of the Damned
Tears of a Clown
The Red and the Black
The Trooper
Powerslave
Death or Glory
The Book of Souls
Hallowed Be Thy Name
Fear of the Dark
Iron Maiden
The Number of the Beast
Blood Brothers
Wasted Years

Madison Square Garden during their World Piece tour, New York, New York, October 8, 1983

DISCOGRAPH

STUDIO ALBUMS

Iron Maiden
Killers,
The Number of the Beast,
Piece of Mind,
Powerslave,
Somewhere in Time,
Seventh Son of a Seventh Sun,
No Prayer for the Dying,
Fear of the Dark,
The X Factor,
Virtual XI,
Brave New World
Dance of Death,
A Matter of Life and Death,
The Final Frontier,
The Book of Souls,

UK April 1980, No 4; US August 1980, did not chart
UK February 1981, No 12; US June 1981, No 78
UK & US March 1982, No 1 (UK); No 33 (US)
UK & US May 1983, No 3 (UK); No 14 (US)
UK & US September 1983, No 2 (UK); No 21 (US)
UK & US September 1986, No 3 (UK); No 11 (US)
UK & US April 1988, No 1 (UK); No 12 (US)
UK & US October 1990, No 2 (UK); NO 17 (US)
UK & US May 1992, No 1 (UK); No 12 (US)
UK & US October 1995, No 8 (UK); No 147 (US)
UK & US March 1998, No 16 (UK); No 124 (US)
UK & US May 2000, No 7 (UK); No 39 (US)
UK & US September 2003, No 2 (UK); No 18 (US)
UK August 2006, No 4; US September 2006, No 9
UK & US August 2010, No 1 (UK); No 4 (US)
UK & US September 2015, No 1 (UK); No 4 (US)

SINGLES

Running Free,
Sanctuary,
Women in Uniform,
Twilight Zone,
Purgatory,
Run to the Hills,
The Number of the Beast,
The Flight of Icarus,
The Trooper,

UK February 1980, No 34
UK May 1980, No 29
UK October 1980, No 35
UK March 1981, No 31
UK June 1981, No 52
UK Feb 1982, No 7; US No 100
UK April 1982, No 18
UK August 1982, No 7
UK June 1983, No 12

② Minutes to Midnight,	UK August 1984, No 11
Aces High,	UK October 1984, No 20
Running Free (live)	UK September 1985, No 9
Run to the Hills (live)	UK December 1985, No 26
Wasted Years,	UK September 1986, No 9; US No 35
Stranger in a Strange Land,	UK November 1986, No 22
Can I Play With Madness?,	UK March 1988, No 3
The Evil That Men Do,	UK August 1988, No 5
The Clairvoyant	UK November 1988, No 6
Infinite Dreams (live),	UK November 1989, No 6
Holy Smoke,	UK September 1990, No 3
Bring Your Daughter...to the Slaughter,	UK December 1990, No 1
Be Quick or be Dead,	UK April 1992, No 2
From Here to Eternity,	UK June 1992, No 21
Wasting Love,	UK September 1992, did not chart
Fear of the Dark (live)	UK March 1993, No 5
Hallowed Be Thy Name (live),	UK October 1993, No 9
Man on the Edge,	UK September 1995, No 10
Lord of the Flies,	UK April 1996, did not chart
Virus,	UK September 1996, No 16
The Angel and the Gambler,	UK March 1998, No 18
Futureal,	UK July 1994, did not chart
The Wicker Man,	UK April 2000, No 9
Out of the Seventh Planet,	UK October 2000, No 20
Run to the Hills (live),	UK March 2002, No 9
Wildest Dreams,	UK September 2003, No 6
Rainmaker,	UK November 2003, No 13
The Number of the Beast (live)	UK January 2005, No 2
The Trooper (live)	UK August 2005, No 5, US No 67
The Reincarnation of Benjamin Breeg,	UK August 2006, did not chart
Different World,	UK December 2006, No 3
El Dorado,	UK June 2010, did not chart
Satellite ①⑤...the Final Frontier,	UK August 2010, did not chart
Coming Home,	UK October 2010, did not chart
Speed of Light,	UK August 2015, did not chart
Empire of the Clouds,	UK April 2016, did not chart